HIDDEN
HISTORY
of
NATCHEZ

Josh Foreman & *Ryan Starrett*

THE
History
PRESS

Published by The History Press
Charleston, SC
www.historypress.com

Front cover: Library of Congress.
Back cover: *Natchez, Mississippi*. Library of Congress Prints and Photographs Division.

First published 2021

Manufactured in the United States

ISBN 9781467148207

Library of Congress Control Number: 2021937254

This book is dedicated to:

My teachers at St. Richards and St. Joseph Catholic Schools, especially:
Bernie Lieb, who instilled in me a love of learning and history (as well as a fear
of the Careless Error Monster);
Dave Wissel, my confirmation sponsor, coach and mentor;
Brother John Brennan, who opened up the gym most Friday nights, was the first
to welcome me back to St. Joe as a coworker and waited outside with me until
the truck arrived that pulled my van out of a ditch I had parked in at a St. Joe
football game a long, long time ago;
Cleta Ellington, who taught me about the "Hero's Journey" and became one of
my heroes in the process;
and Father Brian Kaskie whose love of sports, books, music and life was
contagious. I'm working hard to get where you are for some more Canary
basketball games and conversations about Michener's books.
—Ryan

To the people of South Korea, who introduced me to some of life's great pleasures:
ice-cold bowls of mul naengmyeon and red-hot bowls of sundubu jjiggae, hikes
under the pines of Namsan, soaks in the tubs of the jimjilbang, bike rides along
the Hangang, and never-ending nights out in Itaewon, among many, many others.
Thank you for welcoming a Mississippi boy into your wonderful country many
years ago.
—Josh

CONTENTS

PREFACE

This work is a collection of ten stories from the history of Natchez. They are by no means exhaustive or definitive. In fact, many of the chapters are open to alternative interpretations, and every chapter can be expanded and improved. It is our hope that these brief stories spark a more general interest in Natchez's rich history and lead to more scholarly development.

ACKNOWLEDGEMENTS

We would like to thank all of those historians, researchers, archivists, teachers, artists and photographers who came before us and paved the way for a project like this. We thank them for allowing us to stand on their shoulders and see the history of Natchez through their own work.

We would like to extend a special thanks to those directly involved in our project—Joe Gartrell, acquisitions editor at The History Press, and Rick Delaney, production editor at The History Press. We would also like to thank Jennifer McGillan and the Mitchell Memorial Library at Mississippi State University, and the pioneering institutions making primary sources, art resources and scholarly work easily accessible from anywhere in the world: the Internet Archive, Wikimedia Commons, the Library of Congress, Smithsonian Institution, National Archives, Metropolitan Museum of Art, Rijksmuseum, New York Public Library, HathiTrust Digital Library, Creative Commons, Beinecke Rare Book and Manuscript Library at Yale University, Ancestry.com and Newspapers.com, to name some we have found particularly helpful.

CHAPTER 1

"THEY WERE DISTURBED BY THEIR CRIES AND TEARS"

The 1729 Massacre at Natchez

MONDAY MIDMORNING, NOVEMBER 28, 1729

He strutted about, looking at the remains of 145 men, 36 women and 56 children. Most were scalped, many mutilated, all bleeding from their newly acquired wounds. He stopped and stood in the center of the ring of corpses, pleased, contented and still bubbling with the joy of a successful battle. He had duped his enemy and then slain or captured all of them…almost.

He ordered his warriors to assemble the dead in a circle, lifeless hands laid on each other, eyes staring vacantly into the void. Now, he paced among them and delivered a harangue-turned-eulogy.

Your death is the result of your arrogance and greed. You came seeking land and trade, and we gave you both. At first, the French and the Natchez lived in peace and mutual benefit. You traded to us what we wanted and we returned to you what you needed. Such cooperation could have gone on indefinitely. But then you wanted more. Still, we treated you as brothers. But then you wanted still more. We forgave you and continued to work alongside you. Still, you wanted more and more and more. Then you insult us and demand from us the holy land of our ancestors, the White Apple Village, and thereby signed your own death sentence. You tried to

"Le transport du Grand Soleil," by Le Page du Pratz. *Library of Congress.*

drive your brothers away, and now you lie here dead, at the hands of your
would-be brothers. You tried to enslave our women and children, now we
carry away your women and children. They will slave for us, and when
the time comes, they will accompany our dead to the Great Village.[1]

The Natchez had sent a message to the Europeans. And it was heard—
loud and clear.

THREE MONTHS BEFORE, PIERRE and Marie Mayeux had set out for paradise.
Or at least Eden. It had not been an easy journey, but they had had little
choice.

Their voyage to the garden that they hoped would be their permanent
home and final destination began in La Rochelle, France, when they boarded
the ship *Le Profund.* The Mayeuxs had decided that their native France had
nothing left to offer. They were poor, were growing poorer and had neither
prospects nor hope for a better life. Consequently, they decided to cast their
lot with John Law's Company of the Indies, which had promised them a
successful, prosperous and peaceful life in the newly established French
colonies along the Gulf of Mexico.

After a difficult, cramped and oftentimes frightening voyage, the Mayeuxs finally disembarked on the scorching, rat-infested, barren Ship Island, their introduction to their New World paradise. Soon after, the couple was rowed over to Biloxi, the capital of French Louisiana. It was hardly an improvement. The capital city was more of a camp, crowded, disease-ridden and populated by the dregs of French society. After only a brief stay, the two finally made their way to the Promised Land, Arkansas Post. It wasn't an upgrade.

After a six-hundred-mile journey, the couple, along with eighty others and a handful of soldiers and slaves, arrived at Arkansas Post. Along the way, Pierre and Marie had stopped briefly at Fort Rosalie, high on the bluffs of Natchez. *This* was the heaven they had been promised. But they continued on.

After spending several years at the crumbling Arkansas Post, the frustrated couple doubled back to New Orleans and, not long after, made their way to Natchez.

Natchez, the "Jewell of the Mississippi," had been simply breathtaking when they had sailed past it years before. The Mayeuxs had seen five hundred happy French farmers living in perfect harmony with five thousand equally contented Natchez Indians. The view was spectacular, the land prelapsarian, the future utopian.

Little did Pierre and Marie know how intertwined their fates would be with the paradise that was Natchez.[2]

Monday, Early Morning, November 28, 1729

Sieur de Chepart, the commander of the Natchez concession, watched as the friendly Natchez chief, the Great Sun, approached Fort Rosalie with thirty of his warriors. They brought with them the calumet, held aloft for all to see, as well as their monthly payments and gifts for the commander.

Chepart heard the drums and stumbled outside to greet his ally and friend. The two—Chepart and the Great Sun—had spent the previous evening drinking, smoking and bedding the native beauties of Natchez. Chepart did not return to the fort until four o'clock in the morning. Now, five hours later, somewhere between a buzz and a hangover, and still wearing his nightshirt, the commander stepped outside to receive his gifts.

"Fell the Shining Hatchets Quickly 'Mid the Thickly-Crowded Women," *Harper's Weekly*, March 17, 1860. *Internet Archive.*

He walked up to his recent drinking and carousing companion, who, in turn, offered the calumet to Chepart. As the Frenchman reached to take hold of the peace pipe, a shot rang out below, along the river. At that very moment, the Natchez warriors stormed the fort. Chepart was knocked down and beaten as the men around him were likewise attacked before they could offer resistance.[3]

The slaughter commenced all around Chepart. At the same time, Natchez warriors, who had been visiting the houses all along the concession under the guise of friendship, began revenging themselves on the unsuspecting French.

HE WAS A TAILOR. He hoped to make a living and then a fortune in the New World. Le Beau was one of two French men taken captive, along with 80 women and 150 children. He was spared by the Natchez because they needed him. They now had scores of clothes, but few fit. Only a skilled tailor could make the necessary adjustments. Thus, Le Beau was spared.

He watched as the clothes were unceremoniously torn off his brethren and then brought to him, some with tearstains, most with bloodstains. He was immediately put to work resizing and refitting the outfits to fit his captors.[4]

Sketch from Oeuvres Complètes by François-René Chateaubriand. *Internet Archive*.

As Le Beau held each individual shirt and pants and blouse, he no doubt recalled the previous owner of the article. So many friends and acquaintances, now, all dead. No, not all; there were still 230 alive. But when they, too, met their end by strangulation or torture, he would be called on to strip the bodies to make a new outfit for the murderers. Day after day, the once hopeful tailor's mind was reminded of the massacre as he worked on one bloodstained piece of cloth after another.[5]

Worse was to come for Le Beau. Not content with using him to make clothes from his dead comrades, the Natchez soon turned the Frenchman into a decoy. When they heard a French voice crying for help in the woods, they sent Le Beau to retrieve the man with a promise to spare his life. The tailor brought the wounded man from the woods and delivered him to the Natchez, who dressed his wounds, fed him and then cut off his head.[6]

Shortly after, Le Beau lured a passing pirogue, paddled by five Frenchmen, to the shore. When the paddlers neared the shore, the Natchez fired on them, killing three and capturing one. (The fifth man may have gotten away.) The newest prisoner was stripped—his clothes going to Le Beau to refit for one of the Natchez warrior-captors—and bound. He was then forced to run around the village. The Natchez ran alongside him, placed their gun muzzles on him and fired charges of powder into his increasingly burned body. It was only the beginning of a long, agonizing death.

> *The Indians immediately proceeded to prepare, in the square before the temple, a wooden frame...when bound, with his two arms extended on the frame, in the Indian fashion, he saw some French women, and called to them to pray to God for him...scarcely had he uttered these words, when the Indians, armed with bundles of lighted canes, began to burn him slowly, applying them to his sides, thighs, breasts, back, sides and face, so that he underwent a long and painful martyrdom.*[7]

Le Beau, the tailor, stood there, knowing that he was the cause of the young man's death.

THE MAYEUXS' DREAM CAME to an abrupt end on November 28, 1729, but not their lives. Not surprisingly, Marie was taken captive. Somehow, so were her children: Francois, six; Genevieve, two; and newborn Cecile. With other mothers and babies being systematically slaughtered, one is left to wonder how Marie kept her family alive and safe. Most shocking of all was the fact that Pierre, too, was taken captive. While the Natchez slew all other French men, they saw value in a tailor—Le Beau—and a carpenter, which Pierre was.

Regardless of motive, Pierre and family were preserved, the only family to survive the massacre and aftermath. The Natchez immediately put Pierre to work carting materiel from the French fort to the Natchez forts that they were building in anticipation of a French counterattack. Pierre was also forced to put his carpentry skills to work strengthening the Natchez forts. It was a cruel punishment for Pierre. Had his family not been alive, he might have preferred death to taking the household goods, furniture and weapons of his friends and carting them to the abodes of his

"Blessed Charles Garnier," from *Jesuit Martyrs of Canada* (1925). *Internet Archive.*

friends' murderers. He also must have hated himself for contributing to the defensive fortifications designed to impede and kill his would-be rescuers. But what choice did he have?[8]

FATHER POISSON HAD ARRIVED in Natchez three days before. He said Mass—the first Sunday of Advent—in the local church. The Jesuit priest intended to return to his post in Arkansas that Sunday afternoon.

However, some sick parishioners required his services. He acquiesced and spent the night. The following morning, Monday, November 28, he walked to the church to say Mass and then deliver Last Rites to one of his dying flock. On the way, a large Natchez warrior charged him and threw him to the ground. The stunned priest shouted, "Ah, my God! Ah, my God!" before his head was removed by repeated blows from a tomahawk. Father Poisson's companion drew his sword to defend the priest but was immediately shot to death by a second Natchez.[9]

MEANWHILE, BACK AT THE fort, Chepart lay wounded, unable to escape and unable to come to the defense of his charges. In less than an hour, nearly every French man, woman and child on the Natchez concession was either dead or enslaved.

But no one wanted to be the one responsible for killing the commander. It was not fear, but contempt, that kept the warriors from delivering the death blow to Chepart. Warrior after warrior passed on the chance to take

"The Natchez," by Eugene Delacroix. *Metropolitan Museum of Art.*

his scalp. Finally, after forcing Chepart to watch as his fellow countrymen were murdered, scalped and beheaded before his eyes, the Natchez located an old man from the lower class of the tribe and gave him a club. The warriors gathered around and watched as the old man gradually beat the commander to death.

Freed from the stain of killing such a despicable enemy, another warrior stepped forward and hacked the head off Chepart's body. He brought it before the Great Sun and set it next to a stack of other severed heads. The bodies of Chepart and the other decapitated French were placed in a circle, holding hands around the chief.[10]

THE WOMEN WERE SCREAMING. Not like the hardened warrior-women of the Natchez, but like White women, French women. Worst of all were those who were pregnant. The wails were intolerable, but there was a way to stop them. Father Philiberts, a Capuchin missionary to the Natchez, recorded the names of the 144 men, 25 women and 56 children slain that November day in 1729. Honoring those who lived before birth, the priest wrote: "Among the number of women massacred there were four women whose abdomens the savages ripped open and whose children… they killed."[11]

"An Indian Surprise," by F.O.C. Darley (1903). *Internet Archive.*

Another missionary priest, Father Mathurin le Petit, wrote to his superior: "[The Natchez] ripped up the belly of every pregnant woman, and killed almost all those who were nursing their children, because they were disturbed by their cries and tears."[12]

In hindsight, those fifty-six babies and children who were brained, clubbed or hacked to death on November 28 were the lucky ones. For many of those captured by the Natchez, the torture would continue for weeks and months.

All of the French prisoners but two were women and children.

ON FEBRUARY 14, 1730, two-and-a-half months after the massacre, the French finally arrived, seeking revenge. The Natchez were trapped inside their fort. The French had cannons, but the Natchez had French women and children.

During one chaotic moment of cannonading, musket fire, whooping and taunting, a number of the captive women took the opportunity to flee. They made a successful escape, arriving safely behind the fortifications of their fellow countrymen. No more slavery; no more rape; no more torture; no more constant fear of death. The mothers were now safe and free and grateful beyond description.

The next morning, these same women awoke to the comfort of freedom. One, and then several, and then all looked toward the Natchez fort they had just escaped from. Hanging over the walls of the fort were the children of the mothers who had fled. They had been tortured and executed the evening before, and now their limp, mutilated bodies lay dangling from the walls of the fort.[13]

"Bienville," from *Colonial Mobile* (1910). *Internet Archive.*

EVENTUALLY, ON FEBRUARY 25, 1730, after three months of captivity, Le Beau; Pierre; his wife, Marie; their three children; and fifty-one remaining women and children were released in a prisoner exchange (facilitated by the French commander Jean-Baptiste Le Moyne Bienville's Choctaw allies).[14]

They had all come to Natchez having been promised paradise. Instead, they spent eighty-

"Outougamiz rechauffe Rene sur son coeur." From *Les Natchez*, a novel written by François-René de Chateaubriand in the 1820s. *Internet Archive*.

nine days in hell. But, because of their courage, resiliency and tenacity, the survivors of the Natchez Massacre of 1729 were given a second chance at life.

The future success, nay the survival, of Mississippi depended on what they, and thousands of equally courageous, resilient and tenacious adventurers, colonists and slaves, did with it.

Chapter 2

The Man Who Loved His King

Natchez Loses a Father

The year was 1778, and John Blommart was back where he felt most comfortable: on the water, commanding a boat, in service of his King.

Of course, more than a decade had passed since Blommart was a captain in the Royal Navy, commanding a warship in defense of Pensacola. No, these were not the high seas Blommart was plying, and this boat was no ship of the line. Rather, Blommart commanded a modest river-going craft laden with gift goods. The boat, which Blommart described as a "petit augur," had sails and six oars and was crewed by six men.

Blommart and his crew had been traveling for 107 days, moving their little craft up the Mississippi River toward "the Arcansaws"—a geographic denotation that Blommart used for the area where the present-day states of Arkansas, Missouri, Illinois and Kentucky converge. Blommart had covered nearly 450 miles, and he was ready to deliver the cargo he believed would help his country end the American insurrection.

Blommart, a British patriot since childhood, had jumped at the opportunity to help his country on a front far removed from the war-torn Northeast: the Mississippi Valley. He had retired from military life after more than two decades in the Royal Navy, settling on a huge plot of land in the Natchez District—then part of British West Florida—where he farmed, distilled, traded and grew rich. But war in the colonies stirred his sense of duty.

Life on the Indian frontier had allowed Blommart to learn Indian languages and customs, and he had cultivated friendships with the tribes

A Royal Navy captain in the eighteenth century. *Internet Archive.*

he came into contact with. The Crown granted him the title of Assistant Commissary of Indian Affairs, one of many titles he would assume in his life. It was natural, then, that Blommart be the one to try to bring the tribes along the Mississippi River into service for the Crown.[15]

Colonel John Stuart, who served the Crown as Superintendent of Indian Affairs in the South, tasked Blommart with journeying to the Arcansaws to contact several Indian tribes that had recently been "seduced" by the Spanish (who supported the American rebellion and would declare war on Britain the following year). The tribes included the Piorian, Cascaskia, Delaware and Arcansaw (a name used then for the Quapaw). In those days, the Mississippi River divided two colonial giants: Britain on the east and Spain on the west. The two nations vied for the loyalty of the tribes along the river, offering them land and gifts. Tribes would sometimes agree to relocate to one side of the river or the other to demonstrate their loyalty. Blommart was to deliver his goods to the tribes on the east side, in the area then called the Virginia Province, which extended from the Atlantic coast to the Mississippi and began at the present-day border of Kentucky and Tennessee, just south of the point where the Ohio River flows into the Mississippi.[16]

His boat was laden with the sundries Indians loved best. Much of the cargo was fashion items: blankets, hundreds of yards of twenty-four kinds of colorful cloth from around the world, gloves, handkerchiefs, necklaces, combs, buttons, garters and hats. He carried tools: saws, hammers, awls, wire, fishhooks and beaver traps. He had packed plenty of martial items: 150 pounds of gunpowder, 280 pounds of lead balls, three dozen guns, tomahawks, axes, knives and spearheads. And Blommart had loaded his boat with liquor. Sloshing around in barrels were two hundred gallons of West Indian rum and eighty-eight gallons of porter.[17]

If Blommart's estimate of distance traveled was correct, he would have been near the border of Virginia on February 12, 1778, the day his hopes of success sank like the lead balls he carried.

It was on that day that, against all odds, Blommart ran into a man on his way down the Mississippi River, a man whom Blommart knew from Natchez: Captain James Willing. Willing, who had not been a captain when he left Natchez in disgrace the year before, now was. And he led a band of thirty-four American marines/pirates down the river from Fort Pitt in Pennsylvania. Willing's mission was to harass and plunder British settlements along the river. Blommart was as loyal a Loyalist as existed on the southern frontier. He was literally engaged in work on behalf of the Crown and carried with him a cargo worth 3,700 pounds sterling, or 600,000 pounds sterling in today's currency. Willing must have felt incredibly lucky to have such a prize delivered into his lap.[18]

Blommart, with his small crew, knew he couldn't resist Willing. Blommart was taken prisoner, and his boat full of gifts was confiscated. He had wasted nearly four months of his life. He had lost a small fortune worth of gift goods—goods that he had paid for out of his own pocket. And he would soon find himself imprisoned in Spanish New Orleans. Blommart, whose life in Natchez had seemed to be going so well just half a year before, now found himself in a lowly position.

He would not stay a prisoner for long, but he would also not know peace for years. The American Revolution would draw him deeper into conflict; by its end, he would find himself an exile—a father of Natchez no longer welcome in the district.

IT IS UNUSUAL THAT John Blommart—or *Jean* Blommart, as he was known in his native tongue—should be a British Patriot. He wasn't even British. At least, not by birth. Blommart was born a Genevan Protestant. He joined the Royal Navy in, as he put it, his "infant years." He was likely in his early teens when he first became a sailor—boys aged twelve to nineteen joined the Royal Navy by the thousands in the mid-eighteenth century. It was common at the time for Swiss citizens to venture outside their borders to make their livings—to trade, labor and serve as mercenaries for foreign governments.[19]

Blommart joined the Royal Navy in 1746 and served continuously until 1764. Though he did not leave behind a memoir of his adventures in that eighteen-year span, he served in the navy at a time when Britain was active in numerous engagements with its European rivals. In 1746 alone, Royal Navy sailors clashed several times with the French: they defended Nova Scotia; planned and aborted an attack on Quebec; landed at and attacked Brittany; skirmished with the French off the coast of south India, at Madras and off the coast of Haiti; and fought a major battle with them off the coast of Spain. The Royal Navy also aided Austria in the Mediterranean, blockading Antibes, capturing St. Marguerite and fighting in Corsica. And those were just the conflicts important enough to be recorded as "major operations" in a general history. During Blommart's time as a sailor, the Royal Navy fought many other battles with France and Spain around the world. He definitely served Britain during the Seven Years' War, service that would eventually lead him to Natchez.[20]

Blommart must have grown into a capable fighter during his time in the navy, because, in 1764, just after the conclusion of the Seven Years' War, he was given command of a warship and sent to defend Pensacola. His rank came with a symbol of his position in society: a long coat and breeches sewn from wool dyed a deep blue. A white waistcoat, brass buttons and gold lace

Right: "Portrait of a Young Midshipman," by John Downman. *Metropolitan Museum of Art.*

Below: "Sea Fight," by Willem van de Velde II. *Metropolitan Museum of Art.*

New England troops disembarking at Cape Breton. The invasion of French Cape Breton was one of the largest British naval efforts of the Seven Years' War in North America. *Library of Congress.*

embroidery added contrast and luxury to the uniform. A black tricorn hat completed the look. Blommart was one of the first British sailors to wear the captain's suit; the Royal Navy had adopted uniforms only in 1748. Though some histories have described Blommart as a "soldier of fortune," that characterization is unfair. By 1764, he had become, literally, a dyed-in-the-wool British patriot.[21]

Britain won West Florida from the Spanish, and Blommart was one of the men Britain came to rely on to keep the colony. He served in Pensacola for two years before being named Agent Victualler for the navy at West Florida. He now devoted his time to supplying ships rather than sailing them. After twenty years of sailing, Blommart had reached middle age and retirement. The following year, he was elected to the House of Assembly. He had a wife and at least one son.

The Crown granted him a lifetime pension of half pay, and in the coming years, Blommart became known as one of the chief merchants of Pensacola. As a reward for his service in the Seven Years' War, the Crown offered Blommart large land grants on the western frontier: one thousand acres at Bayou Sara on the east bank of the Mississippi and one thousand acres at Natchez. Although some veterans accepted their land grants with no intention of moving to the West Florida hinterland, Blommart could not resist another adventure and a chance at cornering a trading relationship with the tribes along the river. By 1770, he had moved to Bayou Sara.

An incident at Bayou Sara brought into focus the dangers of living on the frontier. In 1772, a group of Indians visited Blommart's plantation for the purpose of ransacking his house. One of Blommart's farmhands tried to stop the group and was stabbed through the thigh. According to John Fitzpatrick, a merchant and contemporary of Blommart's who lived down the Mississippi River at Bayou Manchac, Blommart narrowly survived the visit from the Indians. Blommart "was on the brink of loosing [sic] his life," Fitzpatrick wrote to a friend, "and all the mens lives that were at the plantation with him."[22]

The conflict at Bayou Sara may have influenced Blommart's decision to move his operation to Natchez. By 1775, he had relocated.[23]

Natchez in 1775 really was not Natchez; the British did not lay out a town there until the following year. Instead, it was a river landing "under the hill" with a dozen buildings occupied by a "small, motley collection of individuals," as one history put it. Fort Panmure—or Fort Rosalie, as it had been known—stood dilapidated, overlooking the landing. Many more settlers had moved to the farmland surrounding the landing and had brought slaves with them. In all, seventy-eight families called the Natchez District home, and most had arrived in the previous few years.[24]

Within a few years, Blommart had adapted to life in Natchez like the corn that grew in its fertile soil. He acquired property in different locations around the district. He owned 136 acres just three miles from the fort, where he likely spent most of his time. He had a house there with a barn, kitchen, outhouses, garden and orchard. He built a country house about fifteen miles from the landing that would come to be known as "Mount Locust" (and still stands today). He maintained a house and store at the river landing. At his store he sold smoked beef, hams and bacon, sugar, tools and liquor. He owned two stills—one capable of holding 160 gallons—and produced and bottled rum and other spirits. He filled his houses with fine furniture made of mahogany, cherry and walnut, slept on feather mattresses and ate from china. He raised animals and owned a dozen horses, nearly one hundred cattle and almost three hundred pigs.[25]

Blommart again found himself at odds with some local Indians; part of the land he claimed as his included a peach orchard that Tunica Indians had planted and also claimed. But Blommart also found friends among the Indians, friends who would one day come to his aid by the hundreds.

Those friends were the Choctaw. Blommart supplied them with rum in exchange for bear oil.[26]

He traveled up and down the river, visiting his friend Fitzpatrick at Manchac. He traded for furs, speculated on land and farmed his large plantation with the help of slaves. He became known as the Natchez District's resident scholar and maintained a library of 150 volumes. He had a particular interest in architecture and kept books on design and drafting. He kept mementos of his time as a sea captain, including his navigational charts and maps, a basket-hilt broadsword and a Hadley's quadrant. He assumed another title: justice of the peace. He did what a shrewd Swissman should do, establishing a partnership with a Spanish commandant across the river. The partnership granted Blommart access to Spanish hunting grounds, trade with the Osage and a Spanish passport.[27]

In a few short years he grew rich, well connected and influential. Life in Natchez seemed to be going swimmingly. And then, in 1777, duty called. Blommart decided to support the British war effort in his capacity as a trader, but his capture and imprisonment by Willing put him into a martial state of mind.

By his own words, he "escaped" from his imprisonment in New Orleans. His escape probably resembled that of other British Loyalists captured by

Mount Locust, built by John Blommart around 1780, still stands—incredibly—near Natchez. *Library of Congress.*

Willing and held at New Orleans; they were granted parole and broke said parole, fleeing upriver to Natchez.[28]

After escaping, Blommart committed fully to a new life as an armed resistor of the American Revolution. John McGillivray, a trader based in Mobile, took the lead in organizing a defensive militia in West Florida. He enlisted one hundred British and French, one of whom was Blommart. Most of McGillivray's volunteers came from the Natchez District. Blommart, with his military background and high position in society, was made Captain of Artillery and Barrack Master. Blommart raised a company of artillery. With help from Royal Navy ships and Cherokee and Choctaw allies, the small group of Loyalist militia in West Florida was able to defeat Willing's small force of American raiders. West Florida returned firmly to British control. The Crown stationed seventy-five regulars at Manchac to deter another American incursion, and the Loyalists living there were able to return to a somewhat normal life.[29]

But John Blommart's life in Natchez would not remain normal for long. Blommart and his Loyalist comrades had driven the Americans out of West Florida but would soon find themselves in thrall to a much more powerful adversary: His Catholic Majesty, Charles III of Spain. Blommart would resist the Spanish just as fiercely as he had the Americans—even more fiercely. And he would pay the price for his loyalty to his king.

In June 1779, Spain formally declared war against Britain and set its sights on British West Florida. A young Spanish officer named Bernardo Gálvez was picked to lead an assault on Britain's settlements along the Mississippi. Gálvez assembled an army of astonishing diversity that included Spanish veterans, Mexicans, Canary Islanders, free Blacks, Louisianans, Acadians, Germans and Indians. They marched up the Mississippi, capturing Manchac, Baton Rouge and then Natchez without resistance. They captured three forts, thirteen cannon and more than one thousand British and German troops and militia.[30]

The Spanish treated Natchez's British residents with mildness and respect, granting them rights, honoring property claims and allowing religious practices. The British were also allowed to serve as constables, appraisers and mediators. Though the Spanish won the loyalty of most British settlers in Natchez, some held out hope that the British would recapture Natchez from Mobile or Pensacola, which they still controlled.[31]

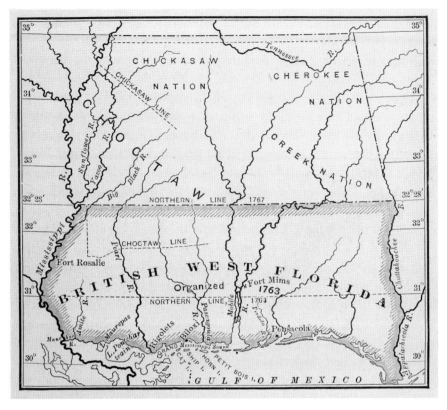

Map of British West Florida, showing the location of Fort Rosalie, the future site of Natchez. *Internet Archive.*

Blommart, of course, was one of those holding out hope of a British reconquest. And he was willing, as usual, to aid the Crown in any way he could.

By 1781, the Spanish had decided to try to expel the British from the Southeast altogether, and their ace commander in Louisiana, Gálvez, led a siege on Pensacola. General John Campbell, the British commander at Pensacola, concocted a scheme to distract the Spanish, save Pensacola and perhaps regain Natchez.

John Blommart would be crucial to Campbell's plan. In order to give the scheme the veneer of a military maneuver, Campbell sent a number of blank commissions to Natchez settlers; they would become British soldiers and lead an assault on Natchez. One of the commissions was for Blommart, and Campbell included additional instructions for the old sailor. He was to raise a corps of volunteers and lay siege to Fort Panmure. Blommart, being Blommart, accepted the orders and went about his task.

He was able to raise about 50 settlers for the mission, but the bulk of his troops came from the tribes with whom he had cultivated relationships. More than 150 Creek and Choctaw Indians joined Blommart. For artillery, Blommart readied two swivel guns the British had taken from James Willing's men three years before and dug up an ancient French cannon from a nearby meadow.[32]

Blommart's men announced their plan to retake Natchez for their king by hoisting a British flag in sight of the fort and firing their humble artillery into the earthworks of Fort Panmure. The Spanish had been informed that a rebellion or military operation was brewing. The Spanish fired back, striking one person, who later died.

Blommart and his men laid siege to the fort for twelve days, with no sign of victory on either side imminent. Instead, if a Spanish sympathizer among the British was to be believed, Blommart's men were near to losing their resolve. The sympathizer, Alexander McIntosh, wrote as much to the Spanish commander inside the fort. But McIntosh's letter did not make it to the Spanish without first being intercepted by Blommart and his men.

And it turned out, ironically, the letter would be the key to Blommart's victory. Blommart and his men set about forging a new letter to the Spanish, complete with a fake signature from McIntosh. The new letter warned that Blommart and his men had tunneled underneath the fort and stockpiled explosives; they were getting ready to detonate the explosives and destroy the fort from below.

Blommart sent his forged letter along to the Spanish. The ruse worked. The Spanish surrendered. Against all odds, Campbell's plan had worked. Blommart had returned Natchez to British control.

Blommart had come through for Campbell, but Campbell could not do the same for Blommart. Pensacola fell to the Spanish five days after Natchez had fallen to Blommart. Blommart and his fellow Natchez rebels found themselves in a cruelly ironic position: victorious and damned, all at once.

Gálvez dispatched a force of 150 to Natchez. Blommart "obstinately defended" the fort for forty-seven days, but with no hope of British relief and an inferior force, he began negotiating a surrender.

Blommart argued that he should be treated as a prisoner of war rather than as a treasonous Spanish subject. The punishment for treason could be as severe as death. But the Spanish would not have it, arguing that he had broken an oath of loyalty to the Spanish king. Blommart and five others were taken to New Orleans and imprisoned.[33]

Before Blommart took command of the Natchez rebels, he was likely the richest man in the district. After his surrender, he lost it all. The Spanish government appropriated all his possessions in Spanish territory, which included several parcels of land at Pensacola, and sold them off. The Spanish kept the proceeds.[34]

In New Orleans, Blommart suffered mightily. In his own words, he was "confined in a dark and loathsome dungeon loaded with heavy irons 22 months during which time he suffered great hardships not only by cruel treatment but for want of Food and Raiment."[35]

Blommart would have surely died of starvation and neglect had a merciful, nameless man not taken pity on him. The man, an English tavern keeper, supplied him with food and other necessaries, keeping him alive just long enough for Gálvez, the conqueror of Natchez, to sentence him to death. Blommart, who had been living in hell for nearly two years, made peace with his imminent demise. And then, his king intervened.

The governor of British Jamaica, Archibald Campbell, let Gálvez know that if he executed Blommart, Campbell would "retaliate." Campbell held Gálvez's own father-in-law prisoner in Jamaica. Gálvez agreed to free Blommart, and Blommart left for Jamaica, a withered shade of his former self, never welcome again in his old Natchez home.

An interior view of Mount Locust. *Library of Congress.*

Blommart made his way back to London, where he petitioned the Crown repeatedly for compensation for the enormous fortune he had lost at the hands of James Willing and the Spanish. He tallied it up to nearly 7,000 pounds sterling, or 1.2 million pounds sterling in today's currency. It is from these petitions that we know so many details about his life in Natchez.

We might be tempted to remember John Blommart as a Loyalist on the wrong side of the American Revolution who received a just punishment for his resistance. But it would be fairer to acknowledge him as a brave, adventurous, capable and curious man with an ironclad sense of duty to the country that made him a sailor, leader and gentleman—and as a father of Natchez.

Incredibly, Mount Locust—a house that Blommart built and likely designed himself—still stands, fifteen miles northeast of Natchez. Visitors can look through the open doorways of the house onto a simple bed frame, a course rug, a candlestick and a writing desk—period furniture meant to evoke the era when Blommart lived.

Absent from the desk are the navigational tools that an old sea captain kept as mementos long after he had given up life aboard a sailing ship. And absent from the bare wood walls of the house is a tacked-up flag: the King's Colours, a salt-stained and tattered banner that once waved at the top of a ship's mast.

CHAPTER 3

TRAVEL RABBLE

Transients in the Frontier Days

In 1796, a bright but feeble young man set his sights on the flowing Ohio River, following with his eyes its path south, and farther south, toward Natchez. The man was Philip Doddridge. He would one day be a famed lawyer and U.S. congressman. But on that day, he was only young and curious.

Doddridge had grown up on the West Virginia frontier. He had helped his family on their farm as a child, but his bright mind and poor health convinced his father to pull him from the plow and put him in school. Latin would be the subject that delighted and intrigued Doddridge, and he was soon conversing fluently with his teacher. When his father said evening prayers, Doddridge would say them after, in Latin. Though he did not know it at the time, his language studies would be the key that would unlock the gates of a town many miles away, many miles downriver.

The area where Doddridge lived, near present-day Wellsburg, West Virginia, sat on the Ohio River. The fertile land produced a lot of wheat, so much that farmers would load their surplus onto boats and ship it downriver to New Orleans. Doddridge's cousins were preparing to do just that and asked Doddridge if he'd like to accompany them. The group floated down the Ohio and then the Mississippi River for thirteen hundred miles. The journey took months and was, fortunately for Doddridge and his cousins, uneventful. Then, they reached Natchez.

The group disembarked at Natchez's little river landing, known as Under-the-Hill. Doddridge, feeling the urge to stretch his legs after the long journey,

"Huntington and the Ohio River," 1880. *New York Public Library.*

began walking up the road that ran parallel to the river, toward the bluffs above—toward Natchez proper. He had made it halfway up the incline when a well-dressed man met him, shouting in Spanish. The man—who Doddridge would learn was the governor of the town, Manuel Gayoso de Lemos—was angry. Boatmen, who had begun floating down the river by the thousands, were not allowed in Natchez.

Doddridge could not speak Spanish, but the tongue sounded much like Latin to him. He tried responding to Gayoso. "Salvē," he might have said. "Quare iratus es?" ("Good morning, why are you angry?")

Gayoso was astonished and delighted to hear the language. He was fluent in Latin, too. The young American and the Spanish governor struck up an instant friendship. Gayoso invited Doddridge to his house and gave him use of a carriage and horses for touring the town and countryside. Doddridge spent a week visiting with Gayoso before returning to Under-the-Hill, where his confused cousins had been "barely allowed to step on shore."[36]

Doddridge's experience illustrated an unusual dynamic that existed in early Natchez. The town was flourishing, in no small part due to bustling trade on the Mississippi. It was also the southern terminus of the Natchez Trace, which nearly all river traders took when returning to their northern homelands. But the men who traveled those earliest of American highways were wild. Boatmen were allowed to stay and revel at Under-the-Hill but were literally forbidden by the Spanish government from entering town. Natchez, whose inhabitants numbered around five thousand in 1797, found itself reliant on the transient workers who passed through—reliant on the money they pumped into the town's taverns and on the supplies they brought in their flatboats. But the residents were determined to keep the men at arm's length.[37]

Kaintucks

The river trade that would bring so many riches and rabble to Natchez was said to have begun in earnest in 1776 with a group of Carolinians. The men were some of the first to travel over the mountains into Kentucky and made their livings off the ends of their guns. They soon amassed a wealth of furs, bear oil and jerked meat and had the idea of floating their fortune downriver to Spanish New Orleans in a crude boat. The plan worked. The men made a lot of money; soon, others were following their lead. Within a decade, more than ten thousand boatloads of frontier goods were floated downriver.[38]

The rough men responsible for ferrying the goods have broadly been called "Kaintucks," whether they originated in Kentucky, Illinois, Ohio or West Virginia. Newspaper accounts of the era referred to them simply as "boatmen." Philip Doddridge may technically have been a Kaintuck while he accompanied his load of West Virginia wheat to Natchez, but he was nothing like the Mississippi River boatmen described, perhaps with some embellishment, by Edith Wyatt Moore, a Natchez journalist who wrote a book exploring the history of Natchez Under-the-Hill. Moore described Kaintucks as nearly subhuman: "Each separate boat was manned by a crew of uncouth, hairy-chested, double-jointed men from the wilds of Illinois, Ohio, or Kentucky." The men were hard workers, hard drinkers and fighters who spoke in a "ferocious jargon full of odd figures of speech and sizzling oaths."[39]

On the river, Moore wrote, the men went shirtless, slept in the open, drank silty river water and ate "unspeakably foul" provisions of jerked meat, salt pork, corn pone and river fish. They were in constant danger of contracting malaria or dysentery, of running into snags that could quickly wound and sink their boats and of being attacked by Indians or bandits who hid in the overgrown vegetation along the river. Often, Kaintucks would hire Indian warriors to accompany them and protect their loads of furs, tobacco, wheat or other goods. Kaintucks would carry their own guns for protection, too.[40]

The life of a Kaintuck attracted those who could not, or would not, accept life in civilized society. Many were former scouts, spies and Indian fighters who found themselves out of work as the frontier became settled. Charles Cist, an early historian of the western frontier, wrote about the Kaintucks in 1845.

Most of them had become unfitted for the pursuits of agriculture—a few followed the chase for subsistence when they could pursue the savage

"Broad Horn, or Flat Boat." From *Incidents and Sketches Connected with the Early History and Settlement of the West* (1848). *Internet Archive.*

> *no longer as an occupation, but of the mass, part had imbibed in the intercourse with the Indians a...contempt and disrelish for steady labor; and the others were...in distress, or in debt, or discontented....They felt themselves scarcely responsible to the laws.*[41]

The boats the Kaintucks constructed for their downriver journeys were crude and temporary, never intended to make the return journey upriver. Instead, they were dismantled at New Orleans after their cargoes were unloaded. They were made on riverbanks, of logs eighty to one hundred feet long. Boards were joined with pegs and sealed with a tarred fiber called oakum. The boats were rectangular and had a couple of oars on each side and one in the back for steering. The boats had cabins for cooking and sleeping. They were large—as wide as twenty feet and as long as one hundred feet. And they could carry tens or hundreds of thousands of pounds of goods.[42]

Because the river was easier to navigate in some seasons than others, Kaintucks would often arrive at their destinations all at once, causing gluts in local markets. In one seven-month period in 1810–11, 1,200 boatloads of cargo made their way to Natchez and on to New Orleans, delivering 130,000 barrels of flour, 600,000 pounds of bacon and 10,000 barrels of whiskey.[43]

"The Shanty Boat" (1891). *Internet Archive.*

Upon arrival in Natchez or New Orleans, some Kaintucks would don a uniform denoting their profession: a blue coat, a red shirt and a coonskin cap. An 1835 description from J.H. Ingraham helps the reader imagine the spectacle an exhausted Kaintuck might have encountered disembarking at Natchez Under-the-Hill after months on the river.

> *The principle street, which terminates at the ascent of the hill, runs parallel with the river, and is lined on either side with a row of old wooden houses; which are alternately gambling houses, brothels, and bar-rooms....The low, broken, half-sunken side-walks were blocked up with fashionably dressed young men, smoking or lounging, tawdrily arrayed, highly rouged females, sailors, Kentucky boatmen, negroes, negresses, mulattoes, pigs, dogs, and dirty children. The sounds of profanity and Bacchanalian revels, well harmonizing with the scene, assailed our ears as we passed hastily along, through an atmosphere of tobacco smoke and other equally fragrant odors.*[44]

The journal of William Johnson, written from 1835 to 1851, provides insight into how Natchez citizens would interact with the Kaintucks who pulled up at Under-the-Hill. Johnson often wrote about how he would visit the landing to buy goods from flatboats moored there.

He usually bought a lot of whatever it was the Kaintucks were selling. On one occasion, he purchased a cartload of coal. On a few occasions, he bought lumber. Once, he bought an enormous amount of provisions: thirty-five barrels of corn, 102 pounds of bacon and one barrel of flour.

Johnson seemed to have made a somewhat personal connection with one Kaintuck who floated his livestock barge down from the Cumberland River in Tennessee. Johnson referred to him familiarly as "the old coloured gentleman." The man's boat held cows, hogs, sheep, geese, turkeys, ducks and chickens. The man had brought his brother-in-law along with him. Johnson visited the flatboat a couple times, eventually purchasing two cows. He loaned his mother money to buy forty-seven geese. The anecdote about the "old coloured gentleman" conjures an image of simple country farmers—like Doddridge and his cousins selling their wheat—rather than drunken and animalistic Indian fighters raising hell Under-the-Hill.[45]

But the roughness of the Kaintuck was a very real issue in early Natchez, as evidenced by Governor Gayoso's strict rules barring them from the town. The most notorious of them was Mike Fink, a sadist and murderer whose infamy grew like a tumor in American lore after his death in 1823. He soon after acquired the status of folk hero (or folk villain) when his exploits were fictionalized and serialized. Moore, in *Natchez Under-the-Hill*, described the man thusly: "Brutish and gorilla-like, with a small head, broad shoulders, and long, hairy arms…he early acquired such primitive protective attributes as sharp eyesight and keen hearing. Furthermore, it was said he possessed the ability to recognize the presence of an enemy by sniffing the air like a bloodhound."[46]

By all accounts, Fink left a trail of misery in his wake and was shot through the heart by the friend of a man he'd just murdered.[47]

Though not as colorful as tales of Mike Fink, an 1817 newspaper account of a brawl at Under-the-Hill provides a look at the very real trouble boatmen caused in Natchez and the effort the town undertook to mitigate that trouble.

A group of five "boatmen from the upper country" was accused of assaulting and wounding a man named James Steward and his son at Under-the-Hill. When a deputy sheriff arrested the leader of the gang, a man named Edward Ward, Ward's friends began to beat the deputy sheriff, rescuing Ward. Although the newspaper report doesn't say how the five men were eventually brought under control and jailed, it's evident from the report that they were. The group was convicted, and the court sentenced the ringleader, Ward, to pay a fine of $700 (around $13,000 in today's currency) plus the cost of prosecution and to spend a year and a half in jail. Ward's four compatriots received lesser sentences.

The Jolly Flatboat Men, by G.C. Bingham, 1847. *Library of Congress.*

The author of the account hoped that the severe punishment of Ward and his compatriots would deter others from committing similar acts, which were "too frequently practiced at our landing," and would show "the firm determination of those in authority to have the laws respected."[48]

ON THE INDIAN TRACE

Though New Orleans was the terminus for many of the disposable boats poled and rowed down the river by the Kaintucks, Natchez was more often than not the starting point for the return journey to the "upper country." (It was possible for men to return to their homes via flatboat, but passage from New Orleans could take up to four months and cost $160 per passenger.) Many Kaintucks chose to make the journey on foot or horseback. The Natchez Trace, which began in Natchez and ended in Nashville (or vice versa, depending on one's perspective), provided the highway for the return journey.[49]

The Natchez Trace was more than four hundred miles long, and much of it ran through the lands of the Choctaw and Chickasaw nations. The road traveled largely through wilderness. An 1804 map of the trace shows the southern leg of the road crossing the "Indian Boundary" around present-day Utica, Mississippi. Around 1800, the United States designated the trace as a post road, and the governor of the Mississippi Territory, Winthrop Sargent, expressed the desire to establish taverns about a day's travel apart along the entire trace. It took five years before the Choctaws and Chickasaws would consent to allowing some of these taverns, or "stands," as they were called by the men who used them, along the road. The stands provided something of a safety net for Kaintucks on the road but were crude even by frontier standards. A traveling reverend described them thusly in 1815:

> *The Indian hotels are made of small poles, just high enough for you to stand straight in, with a dirt floor, no bedding of any kind, except a bearskin, and not that in some of their huts. You feel blank and disappointed when you walk in and find a cold dirt floor, naked walls, and no fire. Camping out is far better than such accommodations.*[50]

Many Kaintucks did camp out, setting pickets at night to guard against attacks by bandits. Kaintucks would begin the journey in groups of fifteen or thirty, hoping that strength would indeed lie in numbers. With few creature comforts available along the way, Kaintucks would carry their provisions and tents with them. Each group would take at least a few rangy Opelousas horses to carry baggage. Well aware that they could be attacked at any time, men took precautions to hide the money they were returning with from Natchez. At least one Kaintuck protected his assets by sewing his money, in the form of four Spanish doubloons, into the waist of his pants.[51]

Kaintucks would sell their goods in New Orleans and return with their pockets and saddlebags filled with coins. The unscrupulous knew this fact and took advantage of the length and desolation of the Natchez Trace to prey on the travelers. The most successful bandits grew infamous. They were the Harpe Brothers, Samuel Mason and Joseph Thompson Hare.

Hare, with his execution imminent in 1818, left behind a confession that revealed the mind and methods of Natchez Trace bandits. Hare came from New York City and was a tailor by trade. He was a small, thin man whose love of fine clothes would eventually lead him to the gallows. He first ventured into the South on a ship bound for New Orleans. He liked the city and found many opportunities for thievery there. In New Orleans, he learned of the

The Natchez Trace the way it may have appeared two hundred years ago, by William Faust. *Library of Congress.*

caravans that traveled the Natchez Trace laden with money. Soon, he was in Natchez with a few companions, and then they were on the Natchez Trace. His first major heist took place a few dozen miles up the trace. He and his compatriots painted their faces with berry juice and stopped a group of travelers just past the Indian Boundary.[52]

A witness account from a later robbery sheds light on the methods Hare and his gang used to halt and intimidate groups of travelers. They would choose a spot on the road and build a split-rail fence blocking passage. Hiding behind the fence, they would wait for travelers to arrive. Hare was armed with a double-barrel pistol and dirk, and he would threaten to blow the brains out of his victims if they showed resistance. He would tell them that he was the devil and would drag them to hell. His blackened face would add an extra element of intimidation to his appearance, though the same witness would later say Hare was not physically intimidating in the least.[53]

In their first heist near Natchez, Hare and his compatriots made off with one thousand Spanish doubloons, gold bars and various other coins worth a total of $13,000 (around $265,000 in today's currency). Hare and his gang preyed on travelers along the trace but eventually made their way to the northeastern cities Hare had come from. After robbing a mail wagon and then splurging on fine clothes in Baltimore, Hare was caught and hanged.[54]

At the southern end, the trace ran through the Natchez District for some sixty-nine miles before passing the Indian Boundary into Choctaw territory. The section of the trace that ran through the Natchez District was policed, and travel there was less difficult. In that stretch of trace, travelers could find a town or stand less than every ten miles. Washington, Uniontown, Selsertown, Greenville and Port Gibson were some of the towns that developed during this period. Though few details about some of the stands in the old Natchez District are known, some of their names have been passed down: Grindstone Ford, Coon Box and Wooldridge Stand.

One of the old stands, a day's travel from Natchez for a Kaintuck, is still there today: Mount Locust, the country home built by John Blommart. After Blommart's expulsion from the Natchez District, Mount Locust was sold by the Spanish government. William Ferguson, a former associate of Blommart's, bought the house. He died, and his wife, Paulina Chamberlain, continued to live there. The house sat directly on the trace, and the owners found themselves, as one Chamberlain descendent put it, "forced to become innkeepers by people who kept knocking on the door." The main room of the house was turned into a taproom, and the grounds were opened to Kaintucks who didn't mind sleeping outside. Around 1799, the Chamberlains built a dorm on the grounds with "two floors of wall-to-wall cornshuck mattresses." Mount Locust survives today much as it appeared in the early 1800s, thanks to a restoration by the National Park Service.[55]

Though Mount Locust had a taproom and corn-shuck mattresses, many of the stands along the Natchez Trace offered fewer luxuries. Food could be had in the form of cornbread, dried fish, pumpkins, mush, potatoes and—if a Kaintuck was lucky—venison. Coffee was available at some stands, along with whiskey or moonshine. A prominent Natchez citizen named Turner Brashear married a Choctaw woman and chose a spot deep into Choctaw territory to operate a "House of Entertainment." Brashear apparently tried harder than some of his peers to make Kaintucks comfortable in the wilderness. He offered venison and coffee at his stand, and travelers there reported that they were "well provided for" but that Brashear "knew how to make a high bill."[56]

The Natchez Trace remained a well-traveled highway for only a few decades. In the first two decades of the nineteenth century, entrepreneurs

Negro Boatmen at Rest, by Rufus Morgan. *New York Public Library*.

experimented with steamboat designs and built boats that could travel upriver without the aid of oars or sails. The Natchez–New Orleans route was the proving grounds for those boats.

Natchez citizens got to witness the advent of an industry that would forever become associated with their town. But the industry would spell the end of the days of the Kaintuck. In 1816, the *Enterprise*, a steamboat built in Brownsville, Pennsylvania, delivered a load of ordnance to New Orleans. The following year, it became the first steamboat to travel upriver from New Orleans to Louisville. The trip, which might have taken three or four months by flatboat, took twenty-five days.

As more steamboats proved that the technology could work on the Mississippi, rates for freight and passage fell to a fraction of what they had been in the days of the flatboat. Soon, boatmen could travel from New Orleans to Cincinnati for just fifty dollars. The trip took sixteen days.[57]

Natchez would continue to receive visitors from the upper country, and Under-the-Hill would continue to be a rowdy place—but not as rowdy as in the days of the Kaintuck.

CHAPTER 4

FROM KING TO SLAVE

The Tragic, Dignified Life of Prince Abdulrahman Ibrahima

Ibrahima's hellish odyssey across the Atlantic finally ended on April 21, 1788, when the *Africa* landed on the island of Dominica. Two weeks later, Tomas Irwin purchased Ibrahima and fifty-six other slaves. The next day, Irwin's ship, *Navarro*, set sail across the Caribbean for New Orleans. Only forty-three slaves would survive the voyage.

The journey across the Caribbean proved to be even harsher than the transatlantic trip. The conditions aboard the one-deck vessels were more cramped. New diseases sprang up. The slavers tried to limit the mortality rates aboard ship by speeding as quickly as possible across the sea. But sometimes, the weather would not cooperate, and the slaves paid the price.

After the slaves spent four more weeks in a deeper circle of hell, the *Navarro* finally anchored outside of New Orleans on June 9, 1788. Tomas Irwin, the slave ship's commander, hunkered down for the next month. It was a wise decision. Although he immediately sold some of his slaves for much-needed provisions, Irwin determined to restore the rest to health. Most, like Ibrahima, had been traveling in hellish conditions for six months. They were underweight, malnourished and sickly.

Sometime in July, the caravan of slaves continued its odyssey. There were now twenty-five to thirty slaves from the original slave ship, *Africa*. They were loaded onto a barge and sent three hundred miles north to Natchez. At last, the slaves disembarked and walked up the muddy, willow-lined banks of what would be their new—and for most, final—home.

Portrait of a West African prince known as Ibrahima, Prince of Slaves, and Abdu-l-Rahman Ibrahim Ibn Sori. *Library of Congress.*

On Saturday, August 16, 1788, a small crowd gathered around Irwin's human merchandise. Ibrahima took in his exotic surroundings. It was day, and the town was crowded. He saw drunks stumbling between taverns along the dirt road; Choctaws in town for business; slaves from the country walking the same streets with passes signed by their masters; farmers and planters visiting the post office, store or racetrack; and flatboatmen loading and unloading their wares. A handful of White men approached Irwin and began examining Ibrahima with sharp and knowing eyes. Five men in particular took a keen interest in the imposing, twenty-six-year-old African. Four of them had no money, only a promise to pay when next year's crop came in—the crop Ibrahima would help pick. One of the men, Thomas Foster, did have money.

The sale was finalized before the Spanish commandant of the district on Monday, August 18, 1788. Foster bought another slave along with Ibrahima and paid $930 for the two. The price was slightly below market value for two young, male slaves. Evidently, the harrowing eight-month, six-thousand-mile journey had taken a noticeable physical toll on the Africans.

When the two slaves arrived at the Foster homestead not far from Natchez, Ibrahima revealed his identity to Thomas Foster and promised him that his father-king would fill his pockets with gold if Ibrahima was returned safely to the land of his birth. Foster scoffed at his slave's pretensions to royalty. And yet he gave his desperate slave a name that would stick with him for the next forty years: Prince.[58]

PRINCE WAS ACCLIMATED TO the concept of slavery. He held a worldview that endorsed the institution. Only now, he was the slave.

Ibrahima's homeland had engaged and profited from slavery for far longer than his new, forced homeland had. Yet, in Timbo, there was a class distinction, and slaves had certain rights depending on their class. Some were semi-free. Others, especially those captured by Ibrahima and his father in times of war, were forced to the fields, where they quickly became acclimated to chains and whips. Even so, the field slaves of Timbo worked

"A New Map of that Part of Africa Called the Coast of Guinea" (1734). *New York Public Library.*

a limited number of days each year; they grew their own foods; they lived together as a group, families remaining intact; and, perhaps most important, their grandchildren had the option of assimilating into the free population. Ibrahima would later explain the difference between slavery in Natchez and in Timbo: "I tell you, [a] man own slaves [at Timbo]—he join the religion—he very good. He make he slaves work till noon, go to church, then till the sun go down, they work for themselves. They raise cotton, sheep, cattle, plenty, plenty."[59]

In Natchez, slavery was absolute: it had come to resemble Dante's hell: "Abandon all hope ye who enter here."

PRINCE SENT MEN TO the fields. He didn't work them himself. He was a Fulbe. A prince of the Fulbe. The son of King Sori. A general and conqueror in his own right. Prince Ibrahima didn't pick cotton for others.

He was familiar with the fields of his new master, Thomas Foster. He grew up with his own slaves planting and harvesting cotton, rice, coffee and indigo. (The latter crop Foster never grew—a fortuitous circumstance for Prince on account of the astonishingly high mortality rate among slaves who worked in the indigo vats.)[60]

Prince was assigned duty as a field slave. Many of the slaves he worked alongside had plenty of experience with the backbreaking manual labor. Many had been slaves in Africa. For Ibrahima, however, the labor was insulting. Almost as insulting as when they cut his hair.

Foster ordered that his new property be cleaned and disinfected. Ibrahima assented. After all, he was a Prince. He had grown up in an atmosphere of cleanliness. He stood there eagerly awaiting his change of clothes, bath and de-licing. But when he saw the shears and understood he was to receive a haircut as well, Ibrahima fought back frantically. His locks were his pride, the mark of a Fulbe prince, a badge of beauty in his native land, and he would fight (and kill) to preserve them. Yet the weakened Prince had too little vitality to resist. He squirmed and fought as best he could but was soon overpowered and tied to a tree. His prized locks fell about his feet.

When Ibrahima felt his head and later saw his reflected image, he realized the finality of his condition: he was to be forever a slave, with the haircut of a Pullo child—the conquered and despised slaves of his native Futa.[61]

THE TWENTY-SIX-YEAR OLD PRINCE proudly rode his war horse. He had served his people well and brought honor to his father. The pagans he was sent to punish were scattered. Several of their villages were burned and their army dispersed. No longer would they threaten his fellow Fulbe tribesmen.

Prince Ibrahima sent his 1,700 infantrymen home; he followed behind with 350 horsemen. He eagerly looked forward to the honors that awaited him back in Timbo, his hometown.

The confident and happy warriors arrived at a mountain pass. They would soon be home, where their women, children and kinsmen awaited. They looked forward to a home-cooked meal, sleeping in their own houses and recounting their recent tales of valor to anyone who would listen.

They dismounted their horses and began to lead them up the mountain. It wouldn't be long before home became a reality.

Then, thunder roared all around them. The sudden cacophony was accompanied by swarms of bees buzzing around them from all sides.

Warrior that he was, Ibrahima quickly understood that he had led his men straight into an ambush. "We could not see them, and did not expect there was an enemy.…We saw the smoke, we heard the guns, we saw the people drop down.…Men dropping like rain.…I told everyone to run until we reached the top of the hill, then to wait for each other until all came there, and we would fight them."

Ceremonie Funebre des Habitants de Guinee (1723). *Rijksmuseum.*

Prince and his personal guard were the only ones to make it to the top. The enemy pursued, relentlessly firing from all directions. "They followed us and we ran and fought. I saw this would not do. I told everyone to run who wished to do so." Some obeyed and reluctantly ran from their Prince. Ibrahima, seeing that the situation was now hopeless, declared, "I will not run from a [pagan]." He sat down on the ground, holding his horse's reins in one hand and a concealed sword in the other.

An enemy approached, gun leveled at Ibrahima. The assailant came to a sudden halt. He had seen that the unarmed man sitting before him was expensively clad. He would be worth a fair ransom price. The soldier hollered at his comrades rushing toward him (and his prisoner) to stand down. He and his fellow warriors turned their muskets around and pointed them stock-first toward Ibrahima. It was a sign that Prince would be spared. An enemy warrior approached him to take custody of the prize-victim. As soon as he leant over, arms extended to arrest Prince, Ibrahima leapt up, grabbed his unexpecting jailor and slew him with his concealed sword. The warrior fell dead at Ibrahima's feet just as a musket butt came crashing into Ibrahima's head. Knocked out, Prince hit the ground, destined to spend the next four decades in bondage.[62]

THE CONQUEROR-TURNED-CONQUERED WEIGHED HIS two alternatives. He could work another man's fields for the rest of what was likely to be a brief life—especially if he was sent to the indigo vats. Or, he could escape. He certainly could not go back to Timbo and Futa. The long transatlantic voyage forced him to reject that fantasy. But he could escape. Somewhere. Anywhere. He could at least live free.

After his hair had been cut, Prince was locked up for three days. His captors believing him acclimated, broken and initiated, he was sent to the fields to gather tobacco. He was to trail a more experienced slave who carried a knife and cut the leaves. Ibrahima's task was to gather the fallen leaves. Back home, the Fulbe scoffed at agricultural labor. Such work was done by the lowest of slaves. Ibrahima would do no such work. He was whipped. Still, he refused. He was whipped again. But his stubbornness and resentment grew concomitantly.

Thomas Foster had made his decision for him.

Shortly after arriving at the Foster homestead, Ibrahima was gone. He left his quarters in the middle of a dark night and fled into the even darker woods surrounding Natchez.

PRINCE LIVED FREE FOR many weeks. The dogs couldn't find him, nor could the trackers. He left no trail, no trace that he had ever been in Natchez. The warrior-prince had simply vanished.

Although his precise whereabouts has never been determined, it is likely that he remained in the vicinity of the Foster farm, for he would return there weeks later, after he had been given up for dead by his pursuers.

Wherever Ibrahima hid, he must have endured an intense struggle, physically for survival, but also internally. Terry Alford tries to capture what these Gethsemane-like moments must have been like for the enslaved Prince:

> *Chilled by the autumn nights and half starved, he hit the nadir of his existence. To be taken from his family and his father's court and thrust into a meaningless foreign bondage was cruelly unfair. He was no slave in Africa, swapping a black master for a white one. He fell from freedom, a stunning and agonizing experience made all the worse because he was a prince, a man "brought up in luxury and Eastern splendour, now compelled to taste the bitter cup of poverty." A primitive future stretched before him at a labor he could not imagine himself performing.*[63]

Morning Start in the Cotton Fields, by Benjamin West Kilburn (1892). *Rijksmuseum*.

Weeks ago, Ibrahima had lain lacerated on his cot, having been whipped for refusing to gather tobacco leaves. Then, he had been faced with a choice: acquiescence or escape. He had chosen the latter. Now, exhausted and hungry, he was faced with the same two choices. Only now, he had a third option: suicide.

Ibrahima had fallen as low as a Fulbe Prince could. He lived in constant shame, and that shame would be perpetual. Suicide could end it all: suffering, humiliation, shame. But Ibrahima was a devout Muslim, and he believed that such an act of despair would disappoint Allah, who would forever shut the gates of Paradise to him. Death would be most welcome, but it could not come from his own hand.

Shortly after his decision to live, Ibrahima was back at the Foster household, a slave, and yet the "master of his fate."

He walked up to a stunned and frightened Sarah Foster, who was sitting alone, sewing. The tall, intimidating African in tattered clothes approached the White woman. What beasts, what pursuers had the powerfully built slave killed to feed himself and elude capture for so long? And why was he back on the farm? What vengeance would he extract for his shorn locks and lacerated back?

In spite of her wonder and fear, Sarah rose, smiled at the perceived killer in front of her and extended her right hand.

Ibrahima, Prince of Timbo and slayer of Fulbe enemies, escaped slave and survivor of the forests and swamps and bluffs and bayous of wild, primitive Natchez, fell to his knees. Instead of grasping Sarah's hand, he took hold of her foot as he prostrated himself on the floor. He placed her foot over his neck.

The message, spoken in Fulbe, incomprehensible in English, was thus: "*Islam*. I submit. I can do no other, for it is the will of Allah. Kill me if you wish. Enslave me if you'd rather. I accept my fate."

And the next forty years of Ibrahima's life began.[64]

IBRAHIMA WOULD SPEND THE next four decades enriching his master, Thomas Foster. Recognized for his intellect and unique skill set—after all, he was a fallen prince, not a conditioned slave—he was given greater responsibilities and freedoms than his fellow slaves. He ran errands in town. He married a Christian slave and raised a family with her. He was trusted and consulted by his master. In short, Ibrahima's life, though a far cry from the splendor of his youth in Fulbe, was more congenial than what most people, Black or White, could expect in the early nineteenth century.

And yet, he was still a slave; a prince turned slave.

On a summer morning in 1807, on the dusty streets of Natchez, a nearly unbelievable twist of fate would change the remainder of Prince's life.

THE WHITE MAN LAY on the ground. He glanced down at his rotting leg. As a surgeon, he knew he would soon lose it. But it didn't matter. He would die first. He was lost, covered in insect bites, dehydrated, delirious. And dying.

The doctor must have cursed his fate and cursed himself for leaving the ship to hunt. He had become separated from his companions and now lay face down on the ground in the midst of a slow, agonizing death.

When King Sori, the father of Ibrahima, learned that a White man had been seen wandering near his territory, he ordered his men to bring him to Timbo. Shortly after, the surgeon stood in front of the king. No, he had not been dipped in milk as a child. Yes, he was born of a woman. No, he did not come from the depths of the sea. He was a man who had been separated from his companions and now had nowhere to go. Sori told the one-eyed doctor to stay in Timbo and recover. He would be taken care of and could stay as long as he liked.

Dr. John Coates Cox remained with the Fulbe for six months. During that time, he became close friends with Sori's son, Prince Ibrahima. The two would go horseback riding, learn the rudiments of each other's language and pass a fair bit of the abundant leisure time both had together.

Finally, after he healed enough to travel again, Dr. Cox went before Sori and asked that he be allowed to return to his own people. The king granted permission and gave Dr. Cox gold to pay for his passage as well as an escort of fifteen soldiers. They took the doctor to the coast, where he found a ship that returned him to his home in Ireland.

Dr. John Coates Cox spent the next forty years living, traveling and seeking his fortune, all of which he could do because he was free.[65]

In the summer of 1807, Ibrahima was in the nearby town of Washington, Mississippi, trying to sell some excess potatoes. He saw a familiar-looking White man on horseback inspecting the various wares other slaves and Indians were selling. Ibrahima quickly and excitedly made his way toward the man and queried, "Master, do you want to buy some potatoes?" As the man inspected the merchandise, Prince stood by, barely able to control the joy beginning to bubble inside him. Finally, he caught the man's eye. The White man started and then paused. He returned Ibrahima's gaze.

"Boy, where did you come from?"
"From [Mr.] Foster's"
"And were you raised in this country?"
"No, I came from Africa."
"You came from Timbo?"
"Yes, sir."
"Is your name Abduhl Rahaman?"
"Yes, that is my name."
"Do you know me?"
"Yes, I know you very well. You be Dr. Cox."[66]

Left: John Quincy Adams. *National Portrait Gallery, Smithsonian Institution.*

Right: Portrait of Cinque, a slave who led the *Amistad* rebellion and whose freedom was defended in court by former president John Quincy Adams. *National Portrait Gallery, Smithsonian Institution.*

At that, the doctor jumped from his horse and embraced the son of the man who had saved his life twenty-six years before. He impulsively brought Prince to his house. He invited the governor over, too, and explained his own history and that of Ibrahima. Dr. Cox claimed that it was his intention to buy Prince and return him to his homeland.

Unfortunately, the doctor's heart was significantly larger than his assets. Although a kind man and a good doctor, he was not the savviest businessman. Consequently, he did not have the liquidity to buy Ibrahima. Yet, what he lacked in cash he made up for in determination and connections. For the next decade—the last decade of his life—Cox helped to spread the story of the enslaved prince. While he could never offer a satisfactory price to Thomas Foster, who, after all, greatly valued the services of Ibrahima, Cox did introduce Prince to a number of citizens of means. Eventually, the prince's story reached Henry Clay, the U.S. Secretary of State, and President John Quincy Adams himself. (In time, the son of America's de facto royalty met the son of Timbo's de jure royalty face to face in Adams's own office.)[67]

Finally, in 1827, Thomas Foster agreed to free his trusted and valuable slave, provided that Ibrahima return to Africa and that the expense of such a journey not fall on Foster. Subscriptions were raised, and on February 9, 1829, the prince finally boarded a ship bound for Africa, Futa and home.[68]

Thirty-eight days later, the ship, this time bearing an unchained Ibrahima, reached the continent of his birth. But he would never reach his home. He died hundreds of miles from his longed-for destination, a little more than a hundred days after he arrived in Africa. Ibrahima was sixty-seven years old—twenty-six years a happy and esteemed child of Futa; forty years a slave in Natchez; one year a traveling curiosity in the United States, trying to raise money for his return and the release of his family; and three months a free man in the land of his ancestors and happy childhood. But always a Prince.[69]

CHAPTER 5

THE FILIBUSTERS

The Adventures of James Willing, Philip Nolan, James Bowie and John A. Quitman

Throughout its three hundred-plus-year history, Natchez has produced a disproportionate number of filibusters—fortune seekers willing to fight and willing to cross national borders in the process. James Willing sailed down the Mississippi River in an attempt to wrest control of Natchez from Great Britain. Phillip Nolan looked to Spanish Texas. In an attempt to make himself the richest landowner in America, Jim Bowie devised his ambitious and fraudulent Louisiana and Arkansas land grab from the comforts (and debaucheries) of Natchez. From his plantation at Monmouth, John A. Quitman tried, on multiple occasions, to lead a small American army into Spanish Cuba in an attempt to turn the island into an American state.

What was it that drew so many adventurers and filibusters to the city on the bluff, to what was, for a century, the frontier? At one point, "Natchez was the nation's ultimate outpost."[70] It was the "Southwest." Was it the influx of the land-hungry and the desperate—the desperate to win fame and fortune? Was it Under-the-Hill, which lured in so many characters amenable to the idea of profits easily won at the point of a bayonet?

Conceivably, it was the racist *Weltanschauung* that justified demanding the Natchez tribe relocate from their ancestral lands so that the superior French could occupy their hereditary home; that created the nation's second-largest slave market; that espoused the belief that the current American occupiers of the city that had been occupied so many times before had the right to occupy other brown-skinned territories? Or, was it the romance, the history, the promise of adventure that Natchez promised? After all, it was Natchez, even before New Orleans, that drew the adventurous and the desperate to the Old Southwest.

And as Natchez became civilized, these same adventurers sought to extend that wild, barbarous, opportunistic frontier in other directions—namely, Texas, Mexico and Cuba.

James Willing

The rebellious colonies expected an alliance with Spain any day now. Regardless of the lack of a formal declaration, His Majesty had been supporting the rebel troops clandestinely. American negotiators and smugglers had been transporting desperately needed money and supplies from New Orleans to the colonies. But now, that trade was threatened. The British had arranged for their Chickasaw allies to shut down the illicit traffic up the Mississippi River by examining all passing boats for contraband.

James Willing—debtor, patriot and scoundrel—sounded the alarm in the halls of Congress. He stressed the importance of the aid from Spain and the consequent need to keep the Mississippi River open. His plan included capturing several British forts along the great river, including Natchez. Unfortunately for Willing, the Continental Congress rejected his plan. However, a few members, including Robert Morris, gave their consent.

James Willing was born into a wealthy Pennsylvania family. His brother was a partner in the business firm of Robert Morris—the financier of the American Revolution—as well as a member of the first Continental Congress. James Willing was not so successful. In 1774, he moved to Natchez, where he promptly spent much of his inheritance in riotous living. He was a likeable man but a spendthrift and a hothead. As soon as he heard that the revolution had begun, he immediately began trying to win over adherents. He was as unsuccessful a revolutionary recruiter as he was at overseeing his finances. Sometime in 1777, he left Natchez for Philadelphia to offer his services to the cause (and to flee substantial debts that his Natchez lifestyle had incurred).[71]

DOWN IN NEW ORLEANS, Spanish governor Bernardo de Gálvez was excited to hear about the arrival of Colonel Willing. Rumors had reached the Crescent City that a well-drilled, well-outfitted army of one thousand regulars was sailing down the Mississippi River under the command of a capable leader.[72] Although technically still at peace with Britain, Gálvez could see the writing on the wall. In fact, he had already been secretly planning a campaign against Mobile and Pensacola. If the Americans could secure his northern border, all the better.

As New Orleans anxiously—and excitedly—awaited news of the rebel army, Willing did, indeed, sail south toward Natchez—at the head of forty scruffy opportunists intent on plunder.

The raiders landed above Natchez and immediately began a reign of terror. They seized Loyalist property, slaves and crops. They burned food and houses belonging to King George's subjects. In short, they aroused the enmity of nearly every decent West Floridian[73] who now believed that the American cause was one of chaos and anarchy. Many of these dispossessed Britons had no choice but to flee to Spanish territory. Incidentally, Gálvez had to accept the refugees and offer them protection, as Spain and Britain were still at peace.

Willing's raiders then made their way triumphantly into New Orleans. At first, Spanish governor Gálvez greeted them enthusiastically. After all, Gálvez had been clandestinely supporting the rebel cause. Now, here was a way to deliver more direct aid to the enemies of his enemy. He offered Willing desperately needed sanctuary, staunchly refusing to hand him over to outraged British authorities in Pensacola.

Prior to Willing's arrival, scores of British citizens crossed into Spanish territory seeking sanctuary themselves. They told tales of Willing's barbarity. They spread the word that he targeted civilians rather than soldiers and burned houses and farms rather than forts. When the raiders landed and unloaded their prizes, the loot seemed to confirm the accusations. His boats were loaded with captured slaves and precious materials that he planned to sell in New Orleans. And his men zealously guarded their loot.

LEGALLY, JAMES WILLING WAS a rebel and a terrorist. He was trying to free a colonial people from a distant monarch (and fill his pockets along the way). Gálvez himself worked for a distant monarch who feared that a North American colonial rebellion might spread to his own colonies. And yet, Willing was doing damage (albeit minimal) to the king of Spain's historic rival. Willing, therefore, was both a boon and a burden. Consequently, Gálvez offered what he hoped would be temporary sanctuary, and then Willing would be on his way.

The only problem was that the spendthrift, the bon vivant, the bohemian Willing was in New Orleans. *New Orleans*. He wasn't about to go quickly. Furthermore, he began bickering with the American representative in New Orleans about money he was owed. Then he began to get on Gálvez's nerves by constantly badgering the governor for his share of the loot. He questioned the governor's decision to return some of the property Willing had stolen in *Spanish* territory.[74] Willing even

Don Bernardo Galvez, from *A History of Louisiana* (1893). *Internet Archive.*

issued a public proclamation to prisoners Gálvez had already paroled—a clear usurpation of the governor's authority. But whenever Gálvez called him in to rebuke him, Willing was all apologies and humility. And then he inevitably would do something else to annoy his protector. In short, Gálvez couldn't wait to be rid of this troublesome American.

Only Willing wouldn't leave. Month after month, he cited the dangers of travel by sea, where the British navy posed a threat. He cited the dangers of traveling by land, since he would be forced to travel north through the lands he had just plundered. And yet, as each day passed, he was making more and more enemies in New Orleans. But still, he would not leave.

Oliver Pollock, America's representative in New Orleans, wrote to the Continental Congress in Philadelphia, begging them to send an escort down the Mississippi to get Willing out of New Orleans. Eventually, Gálvez agreed to cough up $6,000 to send Willing's remaining soldier-looters north by foot and outfitted a ship to take Willing himself back to Philadelphia.[75]

THE END RESULT OF Willing's raid was the strengthening of Loyalist relations in West Florida to the Crown, the reinforcing of Pensacola and four hundred German mercenaries under British control being sent to the Natchez area to protect British subjects there. The trade along the Mississippi River that Willing had claimed was essential to the Patriot cause—and that was the primary motive for his campaign—was now severely curtailed by the reinforced garrisons at Natchez and Manchac.[76]

"Willing's Marine Expedition, February 1778." From *The Marines in the Revolution* (1975). *Internet Archive.*

Only thirteen of Britain's North American colonies rebelled and declared their independence in 1776. American Patriots hoped all along that eventually Canada and East and West Florida would join the fight and that sixteen stars would be sewn into the national flag. Willing's expedition all but guaranteed that West Florida—and Natchez—would remain loyal to King George.[77]

PHILIP NOLAN

The rugged young man received a letter from Vice President Thomas Jefferson. The soon-to-be leader of the United States had a mission for the Natchez-based filibuster: he wanted to know all about horses.

The vice president's letter to Philip Nolan on June 2, 1798, read:

> *It was sometime since I have understood that there are large herds of horses in a wild state in the country west of the Mississippi, and have been desirous of obtaining details of their history in that State....Your communications will always be thankfully received. If addressed to me at Monticello and put into any post office of Kentucky or Tennessee, they will*

*reach me speedily and safely and will be considered as obligations. As ever,
Your most obedient and humble servant, Thomas Jefferson.*[78]

Philip Nolan had the ear—and the support—of the one man who would soon have the power to actualize both their dreams: the annexation of the Spanish Southwest.

PHILIP NOLAN ARRIVED IN Natchez in 1789 with a letter of introduction from General James Wilkinson to the Spanish governor Manuel Gayoso de Lemos. True to the nature of the ever-intriguing Wilkinson, the letter was in cipher.[79]

It was inevitable, with the patronage of two such luminaries, that Nolan would find success in Natchez. After three years, Nolan left the employ of Wilkinson and traveled to New Orleans, where he received a contract to provide horses to a Spanish regiment being formed in the Crescent City. He would get the horses from the West, in Spanish Texas, which was de facto wild, sparsely settled Texas. The few Spaniards living there were vastly outnumbered by the free, territorial and lethal Native American tribes— most notably the feared Kickapoo and Comanche. Nolan went anyway.[80]

After capturing hundreds of wild mustangs, Nolan fulfilled his contract with Spain. Just as importantly, he brought back a detailed map of Texas, which he delivered to Governor Francisco Carondelet in New Orleans. Evidently, Nolan had been doing more than just gathering horses. He then returned home to Natchez, where he sold his leftover horses to Spaniards as well as Americans.[81]

Nolan's contract with Spain carried on profitably until, during the exchange of one batch, he felt he was cheated of his pay. For the next two years, Nolan "went Native," disappearing into wild Texas and living like a Native. Later, he wrote to Wilkinson, the man who gave him his first introductions to Spain.

> *I was a favorite with the savages and Comanches; successful in the chase, victorious in the little feats of activity, but I could not Indianfy myself at heart; the ties that bound me to society, memory supported. I was a debtor; I had been the only hope of a fond parent. Morality at length prevailed, and after two years lost in these savage wanderings, I returned to the Spaniards determined to make another exertion.*[82]

A sketch of Philip Nolan hunting horses in Texas as a young man, by Frank S. Merrill (1888). *Internet Archive.*

Nolan had spent those two years in Texas doing more than relaxing and studying Comanche ways. He was preparing a return to Natchez and prosperity. On his return, he wrote to Wilkinson.

> *I turned hunter, caught wild horses and made my way to Louisiana with fifty head, protected by the Baron (?). Returned again to San Antonio and purchased and caught two hundred and fifty head....I lost a great part of these by the "Yellow Water," sold the best at Natchez and arrived here yesterday with forty-two head.*[83]

When Nolan arrived back in Natchez, he sold his horses and handed over a detailed map of Texas to Wilkinson. Wilkinson, a trusted confidant of Jefferson (despite being a double agent in the pay of Spain), no doubt passed on this knowledge to the vice president. Jefferson had always lusted after the lands to the west, where he hoped to build an empire of gentlemen farmers that extended from sea to sea. Philip Nolan might help him realize this dream.

NOW BACK IN NATCHEZ, Nolan decided to make the beautiful city on the bluff his headquarters. But it wasn't the beauty of the land that made him settle down. It was the beauty of one of the landed: Fannie Lintott.

Fannie might not have been enough to make Nolan settle on Natchez as his base of operations. The city also had the advantage of being on the road to Natchitoches, which, in turn, was the gateway from Louisiana to Texas. And Nolan had not yet given up on his horse business—nor Texas.

On April 2, 1797, Nolan had entered into a horse partnership with John Murdoch. Courting, connected and with an established business, the future looked bright for the young Nolan. Only three things stood in the way of a prosperous, long life: Governor Gayoso, with whom he had had a falling out; Fannie's father; and his own sense of adventure.[84]

Shortly after deciding to settle in Natchez, Nolan wrote to Wilkinson about Gayoso: "He is a vile man and my implacable enemy....The Baron knows him and has done all in his power to secure me from his vengeance. I have, however, my fears, and I yet may be obliged to shoot the monster with a poisoned arrow." The governor of Natchez reciprocated Nolan's disdain. He wrote to the governor of Texas that Nolan was a fraud, a fake Catholic and was inciting the Indians against Spain. (Fortunately for Nolan, this letter was delivered to the governor; but the latter's death just before the arrival of Nolan left the letter unopened until after he had returned safely to Natchez.)[85]

In the meantime, Nolan was once again in Texas, hunting horses—and making maps. His friend, known New Orleans–based schemer Daniel Clark, received the aforementioned Jefferson letter and responded on behalf of Nolan:

> [T]hat extraordinary and enterprising Man is now and has been for some years past employed in the Countries bordering on the Kingdom of New Mexico either in catching or purchasing horses. [He'd soon be] on the Banks of the Mississippi at the Fall of the Waters with a thousand Head which he will in all probability drive into the U.S....You judge right in supposing him to be the only person capable of fulfilling you [sic] Views

as no Person possessed of his talents has ever visited that Country to unite information with projects of utility.[86]

Daniel Clark's reply to the vice president of the United States on February 12, 1799, seems to link Jefferson to whatever schemes Nolan (and Wilkinson and, by extension, Aaron Burr) had up their sleeves:

In the meantime I must suggest to you the necessity of keeping to yourself for the present all the information that may be forwarded to you, as the slightest hint would point out the channel from whence it flowed and might probably be attended with the most fatal consequences to a man who will at all times have it in his power to render important services to the United States.[87]

Whatever arrangement Nolan, Clark, Wilkinson and Jefferson had,[88] "that extraordinary and enterprising man" returned to Natchez in the fall of 1799, determined to make his most ambitious conquest yet: Fannie Lintott.

Fannie was most certainly above and beyond the up-and-comer Nolan. This was, after all, Natchez, where pedigree and lineage mattered, even in 1799. (The fact that only eighty years before that very land was being settled and developed by the rejects and outcasts of France was a moot point.) Fannie's father, William Lintott, vehemently opposed the union. The bold adventurer who had repeatedly traversed the wilds of Texas, stared down death and lived among the Comanche was not going to allow a pampered nabob to tell him "no." Instead, he asked Fannie's father how many Texas horses it would require to buy his daughter. Cast in the role of pimp, William Lintott was understandably furious. It didn't matter. Nolan continued to openly court Fannie. Seeing the inevitability of the espousal—and the ongoing humiliation of having his daughter courted against his will—Lintott finally consented to his daughter's marriage. Fannie became a Nolan in the winter of 1799.

She would remain so for less than a year.

IN OCTOBER 1800, NOLAN told his new, pregnant bride goodbye. He was going to make another expedition into Spanish Texas to make their fortune.

Nolan set out with twenty-one armed men. The new Spanish consul at Natchez, Don José Vidal, asked the United States to arrest Nolan, but because he had all the necessary paperwork—connections—he was allowed to go free. Vidal then told the Spanish commandant at Washita to arrest Nolan, but Nolan slipped the trap.[89]

The rest of the odyssey was the stuff of legend. Nolan and company adventured until they reached the Brazos River, where they found thousands of horses. They befriended a band of Comanches, who promptly stole some of the horses. Nolan, Ellis Bean, a Black man named Caesar and four other men pursued them. Nine days later, they retrieved a number of their horses and returned to the larger company. Unfortunately, the Spanish, guided by some natives, came upon their camp and surprised them. A shootout ensued. On March 22, 1801, Nolan was shot in the head. He died on the spot.[90]

When Fannie had said goodbye five months before, she had refused to consider that it might be the last time she would see her beloved husband and the father of her unborn child. She died never knowing the truth, only what Natchez society told her: that she had been betrayed and deserted. She, Fannie Lintott, who at one time could have had any beau she wanted.

Six months later, her child was born, fatherless. Shortly after, Fannie died. After a brief twenty-one years, the child joined his parents, dying of consumption. He was buried next to the mother who had had such high hopes for the little boy growing in her womb when her husband—the man she had defied her father and Natchez convention for—departed on the journey that would make his family generational money.

That man—Philip Nolan—was buried in an unmarked tomb in Spanish Texas, like so many other Natchez-based filibusters.

JAMES BOWIE

It wasn't the first time James Bowie had been shot. That had been nine months earlier at Bailey's Hotel in Alexandria, Louisiana. Then, he had raised a chair to batter his antagonist, only to feel a sharp pain in his chest. Its sting only enraged him. He leapt on the unfortunate and began beating him savagely with one fist while the other lifted a clasp knife to his teeth and began to open the deadly blade. But friends of his victim leapt on him before the blade locked and he could claim undisputed victory. Nevertheless, he sank his teeth into his assailant's hand as he was dragged away, one tooth still in the hand. He spent the next several weeks recovering. And simmering.

"Bowie Knife," a print by Allen and Ginter's Cigarettes (1887). *Metropolitan Museum of Art.*

And plotting. He vowed never to be in this position again, bedridden by a bullet. He promised to never lose another fight. He saw that guns had proved unreliable as he looked with contempt at his wound, delivered by a pistol at point-blank range. His clasp knife, too, had failed him. He needed a new weapon, one that would finish a brawl.

While James was recovering in his room at Bailey's Hotel, his brother Rezin brought him a gift: a hunting knife that he had made himself at his plantation forge. It measured one and a half inches wide and just over nine inches long. It was not attractive, but it was deadly and was soon to be both effective and, ultimately, the stuff of legend.

Bowie's knife would accompany him wherever he went.[91]

BOWIE'S KNIFE WAS WITH him when he fought one of the most famous duels in American history on a sandbar between Vidalia and Natchez. He was supposed to be there only as a witness to his friend's duel. But he was James Bowie, and it wasn't in his nature to sit out a fight. Even after the two duelists agreed to a truce, Bowie couldn't leave well enough alone. Both he and Robert Crain, a member of the rival party, drew their pistols, neither believing the issue had really been resolved. Both fired at each other and missed. It was a fatal miscalculation for Crain, for Bowie fit the description that his friend Caiaphas Ham gave of him.

It was his habit to settle all difficulties without regard to time or place, and it was the same whether he met one or many. [H]e was a foe no one dared to undervalue, and many feared. When unexcited there was a calm seriousness shadowing his countenance which gave assurance of great will power, unbending firmness of purpose, and unflinching courage, [but] when fired by anger his face bore the semblance of an enraged tiger.[92]

Now, that tiger was aroused. He charged after Crain, who, when Bowie narrowed the gap, turned and hurled his empty pistol at him, striking Bowie in the head. Bowie staggered to a tree trunk and held on to balance himself. One of Crain's friends, Norris Wright (who had shot Bowie at Bailey's Hotel in Alexandria), sensing that the wounded tiger was vulnerable, walked toward him, pistol drawn. At that very moment, one of Bowie's friends managed to pass him a gun. The two fired and missed, but then Wright drew a second loaded pistol to which Bowie had no answer. However, a friend jumped between the two, grabbed Bowie by his coat and begged him to end the affair. At that moment, Wright fired. The bullet ripped off the friend's middle finger and went into Bowie's lung. If the tiger was angry before, he was in a blood rage now. He tossed his friend aside and chased after Wright. As he reached out to grab his prey, two of Wright's friends fired on him and another bullet entered Bowie's thigh.

With Bowie once again on the ground, Wright and one of his comrades drew their cane swords and charged. They repeatedly stabbed at a flailing Bowie who was doing everything he could to defend himself with his left hand and his famous knife. One sword was thrust into that left hand; another bent as it struck his chest and slid to his ribs. It appeared as if Bowie had fought his last duel.

But at that very moment, Bowie somehow sat up and grabbed Wright by the collar. When Wright instinctively backed up, he unwittingly pulled Bowie up, who then whispered into his ear, "Now, Major, you die!" Bowie then plunged his knife into the chest of Wright and "twisted it to cut his heart strings." The major died almost instantly, falling on top of and pinning Bowie to the ground. Alfred Blanchard then continued to stab at the trapped Bowie until one of the latter's friends rushed up and shot Blanchard in the arm. Bowie tossed Wright off of him and ended the duel with one final swipe of his knife into Blanchard's side, wounding him badly.

With at least two bullets and seven sword wounds, plus the gash on his head from the thrown pistol, Bowie was moved to a hotel in Vidalia, just across from Natchez. Both his surgeon and Natchez gossip reported that he had not long to live. Bowie, however, had other intentions. He thanked his assailants for filling their pistols with so much powder that the balls went completely through him. Within days, the jovial tiger had become a national celebrity. After two months of a painful but good-natured recovery, he was once again prowling his old haunts in Natchez.[93]

James Bowie, from *Texas* (1897). *Internet Archive.*

JAMES BOWIE NEVER SETTLED down anywhere for long, but there were two cities he repeatedly returned to: New Orleans and Natchez.

After a childhood on the move, Bowie spent his early manhood in and near Rapides Parish, Louisiana. However, he had larger aspirations—much larger. Rapides was a place where he could run his schemes and make his fortune. But it was not the social mecca that a transient, garrulous, sociable would-be gentleman wanted to remain in indefinitely. Acquiring land was one thing. Having the patience to develop it and work it was another. Bowie needed excitement. So, year after year, he made New Orleans his winter quarters. And he made it to Natchez as often as he could.

In both cities, he found carnal pleasures but also the connections required to forge an empire.

JAMES BOWIE PLANNED TO become the wealthiest man in the Southwest. He very nearly achieved it. He was a daring visionary with an uncanny ability to locate good land and buy it—illegally. In fact, Bowie operated one of the biggest land frauds in American history. Time and time again, he would find some valuable land along a bayou and then forge some documents, pay witnesses to verify his claims, bribe public officials and intimidate others.

Bowie was very successful. And very greedy.

Before his would-be empire fell apart, Bowie had laid fraudulent claim to 160,000 prime acres in Louisiana and Arkansas. Had he succeeded, he would have owned 250 square miles of bayou or riverfront property and another 200 square miles in Arkansas. James Bowie would have been the largest landowner in the United States.[94]

SCHEMING HAD ALWAYS BEEN in Bowie's blood. He had plenty of land; he just didn't want to work it. The tedium of becoming landed gentry bored him. Instead, he craved action. As a result, his wealth came to him through various nefarious means.

One of his early ventures was to partner with the Laffite brothers, Jean and Pierre, and smuggle slaves into U.S. territory. (The international slave trade had been banned in 1808, thereby driving up the price of domestic—and smuggled—slaves.) The pirate brothers built a holding pen large enough to contain 650 slaves on the Spanish side of the Sabine River. Smuggling the slaves into U.S. territory, along with its concomitant perils, would fall on those willing to take the risk. Drivers like James and his brother, Rezin, would buy slaves at one dollar per pound from the Laffites and bring them into American territory, where they would then hand the merchandise over to federal officials, claiming that they had "recovered" the contraband. When the slaves were sold at public auction, the Bowie brothers would receive half the proceeds as a reward for turning in the illegal chattel. When they bought back the slaves at auction, therefore, they, in essence, paid only half price. At the end of the sale, the Bowies would be in possession of slaves bought well below market value. More important, the slaves would now be laundered and entirely legal, with the accompanying paperwork. Selling them on to a local planter would now be easy. With each slave sold thusly, the brothers received hundreds of dollars in profit.[95]

EVENTUALLY, BOWIE'S SCHEMING CAUGHT up to him. His land fraud had been exposed by zealous federal land agents in Louisiana and Arkansas and by suspicious judges, while his slave laundering had become too dangerous. It was time to move on. By 1830, Bowie had decided to make a permanent move to Texas.[96] He went to Natchez to settle some business (and to play faro, drink and boast) and asked that $10,000 be forwarded to him once he reached Saltillo. After ten years of trying to make his fortune through various scams and swindles in the United States, Bowie finally decided to throw in the towel and try his luck in Mexican Texas.[97]

Six years later, his luck would run out at a church in San Antonio known to history as the Alamo. James Bowie, counterfeiter, duelist, swindler and slavedriver, would also be known to history as one of the heroes who gave his life for liberty.

JOHN A. QUITMAN

Venezuelan-born General Narciso López was determined to drive the Spaniards out of Cuba. Mississippi governor John A. Quitman was determined to bring Cuba under American rule. The two decided to become unlikely allies.

Fifty-three-year-old López had served Spain as a soldier and an administrator for more than three decades. He had even served as the assistant to the capitan general of Cuba. But when his boss had been replaced and he lost a good deal of money in several failed business ventures, López became a virulent anti-Spanish agitator. Forced to flee to the United States, he began to make plans to return and liberate the island. With men like himself in charge, he foresaw a strong and mutually beneficial relationship—built on slavery—with the southern United States. Perhaps Cuba might one day be admitted as a state in much the way Texas had—again, with himself as one of the island's leaders.

López took his proposal to Jefferson Davis and Robert E. Lee, both of whom considered the proposition but respectfully declined. He then approached Governor John A. Quitman, who saw the logic behind a Deep South–Cuba alliance. From Natchez, the governor wrote to his former Mexican War aide Mansfield Lovell: "Your old commander is invited to become the Liberator of a beautiful and rich island in the Gulf….My spirit often reverts to the free air of the camp. I am by nature a soldier. No other life charms me."[98]

López's proposed filibuster was not the first time that Quitman had been tempted with dreams of building a slave empire to the south of his beloved South.[99]

QUITMAN HAD SOLIDIFIED HIS expansionist philosophy during the Mexican War, where he served as both a general and a provisional governor of the country. Exposed to the beauty and potential of Mexico, he wrote home to his wife in Natchez that America should "make this beautiful & rich country a portion of the United States." At the same time, from his command center in Mexico, he wrote home to Senator Henry Foote: "I speak to you boldly, as *we* spoke when the Texas question arose, hold on to this country. It is destiny, it is ours."[100] So adamant was Quitman that the United States annex Mexico, that in 1848, the Democratic Party—of which so many members shared similar sentiments—nearly nominated him to run as their presidential candidate. (In a close convention election, Quitman just missed receiving the nomination. He would once again become a candidate in 1855: "Douglas and Quitman, for President and Vice-President.…Place at the masthead of the old Democratic ship, a flag bearing the names and watchwords. Douglas, Quitman, Kansas, Nebraska and Cuba.")[101]

With the arrival of López in 1848, Quitman now had an outlet for his dreams of an extended southern empire.

Honorable John A. Quitman of Mississippi (1855). *Library of Congress.*

López quickly put together a force of adventurers, and his expedition was scheduled to leave New Orleans for Cuba on May 1, 1850. Quitman agreed to take command of a second wave of filibusters, on one condition: that the beachhead already be established and that the Cuban people rally en masse to López's cause. Should the revolution get off to such an auspicious start, Quitman would leave his native Natchez and establish himself as ruler of Cuba. Clearly, Quitman was hedging his bets by insisting that the revolution already be underway—and successfully so—before he committed himself. However, he was confident enough to write his old and trusted comrade Lovell, suggesting that he join him and become his prime minister or secretary of war.

López's expedition did indeed set off in May 1850. While he awaited news of the filibuster, Quitman made a weeklong tour of one of his plantations in Holmes County. When he returned to the governor's mansion, he learned of the disaster in Cuba. López and 520 men had landed on the Cuban coast and attacked a small garrison at Cárdenas. His intention was to take the fort and march on Havana. But the fort's defenders didn't cooperate. They killed 60 of his men before he finally took the town. The delay had cost him dearly, and the Cubans he was counting on never materialized. In fact, many joined the Spanish side against him. López had no choice but to flee to Key West, Florida. Needless to say, Quitman would not become ruler of Cuba in 1850.[102]

Nor would Quitman assume command of the island in August 1851, when López made a second attempt to take the isle.

López's second filibuster was far more disastrous. Just like the first, the Cuban people never flocked to his standard.[103] When he divided his forces, he became an easy quarry for the well-prepared and superior Spanish forces. The filibusters were rounded up and either killed in battle, sentenced to hard labor or executed. López himself was publicly hanged in Havana.[104]

Meanwhile, back in Natchez, Quitman had been charged with breaking the neutrality laws by aiding and abetting an illegal filibuster. He was threatened by the federal government with arrest and informed that the marshal of Mississippi would escort him to trial in New Orleans. Naturally, Quitman was outraged and threatened to call out the Mississippi militia. With a civil war on the horizon, Quitman finally agreed to play the role of southern-rights martyr, resign the governorship and submit to arrest.

After three hung juries, the prosecutor decided to drop the case. The New Orleans newspapers published the following telegram from Natchez, dated March 8, 1851: "So great was the joyful excitement in Natchez last night on the termination of the Cuban humbug in your city, that the night was made voiceful with the roar of cannon. Fifteen guns were fired for Quitman and fifteen for (the) Southern States. Many persons pulled off their stockings [*sic*] for cartridges, and fired several for mankind in general."[105]

Natchez's hero, and the champion of states' rights, returned home in triumph, with Cuba and empire still on his mind. His plantation at Monmouth would become the de facto headquarters of a final attempt to take the Pearl of the Antilles.

ALTHOUGH THE 1850 AND 1851 invasions ended in unmitigated disaster, Quitman wasn't ready to give up on Cuba. When President Franklin Pierce appointed Jefferson Davis as his secretary of war and filled other important posts with pro-filibuster appointees, Quitman decided the time was finally right to annex Cuba as another slave state. On April 29, 1853, a group of revolutionaries arrived in Natchez and offered Quitman supreme command of their upcoming expedition. He eagerly accepted the offer.

Quitman spent the next several months ensuring that the administration in Washington would remain sympathetic to his undertaking and planning the invasion itself. From his plantation at Monmouth and during frequent visits to New Orleans, he assembled a "gentlemen's" expedition.

Quitman began to work more hurriedly when he learned that Spain, under pressure from Great Britain, was considering full-scale emancipation. It had already freed a large percentage of the island's Black population that had been brought to the island illegally from the United States. If Cuba became a free country, conquering it on behalf of the United States would do Quitman and the South no good, as it would inevitably then enter the Union as another free state. In addition, a Cuba composed of so many free Blacks, so close to the Gulf Coast, would be a constant thorn in the side of the pro-slavery cause, not to mention a source of inspiration to any would-be slave rebellions in the southern states. The rebellion in Santo Domingo had terrified southern slaveholders. Yet another successful, predominately Black nation so close to home was unthinkable to Quitman and his associates. Natchez's *Free Trader* described an Africanized Cuba as "too terrible to be contemplated without a shudder."[106]

Time was running out on Quitman's dreams of expanding the peculiar institution that he had sworn to not only defend but also expand.

If Spanish emancipation went through, annexing Cuba would no longer be enticing to southerners, who would inevitably lose even more power in Congress. If the United States bought Cuba from Spain, the island would be held in territorial status until the more powerful northern states could shape its state constitution. And if America invaded and annexed Cuba, the authorities almost certainly would free the island's Blacks to fight against the *norteamericanos*.[107]

Consequently, Quitman needed to conquer the island as swiftly as possible, while slavery was still intact, and hand it over to the United States as a slave state. Any other scenario would be self-defeating. Quitman, after all, had already helped Texas do exactly that. The blueprint was already prepared; the filibusters just needed to conquer the island.

THE GOVERNOR'S PROGNOSTICATIONS OF doom resonated throughout the South. The threat of a new "mongrel empire"—Spain had just legalized mixed marriages—so close to the border, as well as the need to add as many representatives as possible to Congress to ensure that slavery would continue to be protected, sent throngs of adventurers to Quitman's recruiters. In fact, so many tried to enlist that Quitman was able to be quite selective with those he took on board. Aside from the expected Cuban expatriates who wanted to see slavery perpetuated on their island, Quitman added judges, college students, U.S. Army personnel, planters, newsmen, congressmen, a bank president, a former and an acting governor, lawyers, state legislators and previous filibusters to his role of supporters, many of whom planned to enlist themselves when the expedition was finally underway. It was truly "a gentlemen's expedition."[108]

Finally, by February 1855, everything seemed ready. Quitman had several thousand men and a war chest of $500,000. The invasion was planned for the first week of March. By then, it was expected that Cuba would be in the midst of a two-week-old revolution, sparked by the assassination of the island's leader while he attended an opera.

Unfortunately for Quitman, it seemed as if the entire country—in fact, both countries—knew of the filibuster. A newsman even tracked down the filibuster camp as they awaited their ships. He was sure to let the rest of America know what was going on. And, of course, Spain had her own spies as well, keeping the Cuban government updated on the imminent expedition. They kept an extra-vigilant eye on Quitman, for everyone knew he would be leading the invasion.

Cuba itself was placed under martial law as the island awaited Quitman's first move. A British admiral wrote of Cuba in early 1855: "[The Cuban captain-general] has given me to understand…he had reason…to expect the arrival of a filibustering expedition under Colonel Quitman,—and certainly since my arrival there have been some symptoms of activity with the Spanish squadron and troops. A frigate, two brigs and three steamers have gone to sea."[109]

More ominously for Quitman, President Franklin Pierce—who had given his tacit approval, provided Quitman remain under the radar—had been forced by Congress and the press to crack down on filibustering. One of Quitman's ships in New Jersey that had been loaded with weapons and supplies was seized. Incensed, Quitman made his way to D.C. to confront Pierce. He ran into the president while walking along Pennsylvania Avenue. Pierce tried to brush him off but acquiesced to meet with him at the White House. When Quitman showed up, he was greeted by the president along with the secretary of state and the Spanish minister to the

The Monmouth House in Natchez, home of John A. Quitman. *Library of Congress.*

United States. It proved to be an ominous gathering. Pierce said that he could no longer even privately endorse the filibuster. He also shared his knowledge of Cuba's substantial preparations to greet Quitman when he finally arrived on the island.

Lack of support at home and a vigilant enemy convinced Quitman to finally abandon his career as a filibuster—at least actively. He would go to his grave calling for the annexation of Cuba and other Caribbean and Latin American countries in order to preserve the "southern way of life." He would continue to call upon the "Caucasian white race to carry humanity, civilization, and progress to the rich and fertile countries to the south of us, which now, in the occupation of inferior and mixed races, lie undeveloped and useless."[110]

John A. Quitman would die in Natchez in 1858, an unrepentant, spiritual filibuster to the end.

THREE YEARS LATER, QUITMAN—AND Willing's and Nolan's and Bowie's—Natchez, along with the rest of Mississippi, attempted the filibusters' ultimate fantasy: the acquisition of a 770,400-square-mile territory conquered and ruled by an elite few.

The filibuster ended as an unmitigated failure in 1865.

CHAPTER 6

"THERE'S A BETTER DAY A COMING"

The Natchez Slave Trade

See these poor souls from Africa
Transported to America;
We are stole, and sold to Georgia
Will you go along with me?
We are stolen, and sold to Georgia—
Come sound the jubilee!

See wives and husbands sold apart,
Their children's screams will break my heart;—
There's a better day a coming—
Will you go along with me?
There's a better day a coming,
Go sound the jubilee!

O' gracious Lord! When shall it be,
That we poor souls shall all be free?
There's a better day a coming—
Will you go along with me?
There's a better day a coming,
Go sound the jubilee![111]

THE MAN LAY CHAINED to the ankle of a fellow slave on a swiftly moving
ship. The roof was a mere five feet above him, so the six-foot-tall slave

could not stand. Twice a day, he was unchained so he could eat and be taken above decks for exercise. The other 170 slaves sang and danced the dances of their native lands. But he was a devout Muslim and refused to dance. A crewman's short-handled whip with a braided leather lash fell on his back, encouraging him to participate. He refused. The lash fell again, to no avail. Finally, he and his fellow captives were again taken below decks.

Once chained to his ever-present comrade, the man looked out the grated hatch he had fortuitously been chained next to. At least he, unlike the slaves around him, had access to fresh air and sea breezes. When allowed on deck, he would be the first to crawl out and the last to resume his cramped berth. Most days, he stared out the hatch and watched the slaver-captain being served tea in the late afternoon.

But the scent of English tea and sea air could not mask the permanent stench below decks. When the bladders of the chained slaves filled, they were released. When their bowels filled, they were emptied. And the excrement sloshed back and forth with the motion of the ship. The almost unbearably hot days intensified the stench. The exceedingly cold nights made them wish for the broiling afternoons.

And the voyage went on, and on, and on. Many of the slaves contracted dysentery and shat bloody liquids for days and weeks at a time. Those unfortunates suffered from intense gut and rectal pains as the ship rolled along the waters. The painful disease caused the chained to suffer fevers and some become delirious. And all the while, they added to the stench below decks.

Other slaves began to develop blisters up and down their legs. Shortly thereafter, guinea worms, which had been living inside the slave and traveling down toward the legs, began to force their way up and out blisters, causing intense, fiery pain as they did so. And still the voyage went on. Nausea, vomiting, the sickly sweet smell of sweat and defecation, the forced dances, the lash, the cramped quarters, the cramps, the chaffing chains. Hour after hour, day after day. Those chained below decks began to eagerly look forward to the auction block and a life of slavery. Many looked forward to death. Anything was preferable to the monotony of the never-ending voyage through hell.

The constant rocking, the lashings, the confinement and the claustrophobic conditions wore on the enchained man. But perhaps the worst pain was the knowledge of who he was and where he had come from, contrasted with who he had become and where he was headed.

Portrait of a Green County, Georgia man born into slavery, by Dorothea Lange. *Library of Congress.*

The man who was born free and familied and loved shut his eyes and tried to ignore the pain emanating from his shackled ankle and the stench from his comrade-in-chain's recent evacuation. He tried to summon dreams of his homeland, dreams of freedom. Instead, he just ached and waited. And waited. And waited.[112]

ABDULRAHMAN IBRAHIMA'S TRANSATLANTIC JOURNEY aboard the *Africa* was not unique. Between the sixteenth and nineteenth centuries, over ten million Africans were herded on to ships and brought across the Atlantic to the Americas. In 1788, the year of the prince's enslavement, 104,040 Africans made their way to the New World.[113]

The newly discovered American continents were full of natural resources. And yet, many of these resources were in subtropical climates, where most Europeans preferred not to labor. In addition, the native population had been decimated by disease and could no longer provide a sustainable labor force. At first, the European nations tried to fill the scarce labor market by

Cotton hoers in the Delta in 1937, by Dorothea Lange. *Library of Congress.*

forcing criminals to relocate to the Americas. Then, indentured servants made the transatlantic journey, but never in sufficient numbers. Finally, European nations came to the conclusion that slavery was the only way to realize the profits that America had to offer.

However, slavery had been abolished in Europe for centuries. White Christians simply didn't enslave fellow White Christians. Nor could the natives of America be enslaved. Aside from dying in pandemic numbers to disease, they knew the land far more intimately than their potential enslavers and, consequently, would simply run away.

And so, a collective decision was made to bring Africans to the Americas.

NEGROES! NEGROES!! I Have for sale, at the Forks of the Road, near Natchez, a lot of LIKELY YOUNG NEGROES. Among them may be found a very superior Blacksmith, a Seamstress, &c., &c.
—*Christmas Day 1850 advertisement in the Mississippi Free Trader*[114]

In 1808, AFTER SIX hundred thousand slaves had already been brought to the United States, the international slave trade was banned. For Mississippi's plantation elite, the timing could not have been worse. The invention of the cotton gin and the steamboat, as well as the introduction of a superior strain of Mexican cotton and the acquisition of Choctaw and Chickasaw territory, made cotton an exceedingly valuable crop. The Natchez elite immediately began converting their farms and plantations into vast cotton fields. Agricultural crops and indigo saw a rapid decline in production as cotton became king.

In order to fully take advantage of the "white gold," the landed needed slaves. And lots of them. With the Caribbean and African slaves no longer a possibility, the citizens of Natchez looked to the Chesapeake region, where the need for slaves was gradually declining at the same time the number of slaves rose. Thus, many Chesapeake owners began to look for a market in which to unload their chattel. Natchez was only too happy to provide one.

Several slave corrals sprang up in and around Natchez. But soon the majority of transactions were taking place at the busy intersection on Liberty Road and Washington Road.[115] The market became the infamous "Forks of the Road."

Two men in particular took advantage of the low cost of Chesapeake slaves and the high price paid by planters in New Orleans and Natchez. By the 1830s, Isaac Franklin and John Armfield forged an alliance in which Armfield would manage slave pens in Alexandria, Virginia, and send them south to his partner. He in turn would store them in his own pens at Forks of the Road before selling them to Deep South planters. Over 1,000 slaves a year made the one-thousand-mile journey from Virginia to Natchez via the Natchez Trace. The men were generally shackled together as armed guards encouraged them along with guns and whips. Other slaves were sent by steamship, 75 to 150 at a time, to the port of New Orleans and then upriver to Forks of the Road.

Armfield and Franklin were not the only two traders to utilize Forks of the Road. At any given time, five hundred slaves would be sprawled about the area in a series of low buildings that resembled a prison camp. Prospective

Portrait of Bob Lemmons, born into slavery in Texas around 1850, by Dorothea Lange. *Library of Congress.*

buyers came and went as they pleased, and pure capitalism determined the quantity and price of the slaves.[116]

Finally, in early 1863, the slave market at Forks of the Road sold its last human persons. The advancing Federal armies soon became an occupying Federal army, and the slave trade in Natchez, and eventually Mississippi, came to an abrupt end.[117]

THERE ARE MOMENTS THAT are either too beautiful or too horrid, that only poetry or poetic prose can put its catharsis into words. Kent Wascom, in his novel *The Blood of Heaven*, describes a coffle of slaves on the final leg of their journey to the slave markets:

> *The blacks came one day pouring down from St. Francisville, ghastly and with dark skin dyed darker from working the vats of indigo....I went outside and saw the tail end of them heading to where the others were huddled at the bank, emptying their bowels where they stood and shivering though it was early summer and the heat was on. They were herded by a man on horseback who stopped at my porch....He asked had I got the contract for shipping them down to New Orleans.*

I said I had, but couldn't take my eyes from them, counting twenty or more of the wretches, men and women and children....The slaves were silent and some had fallen to the ground, unmindful or too weak to care what was expelled upon them by their brothers and sisters. Women holding bony children opened their mouths as if to speak, but only streams of purple vomit fell from between their lips and the held children didn't struggle.[118]

THERE WERE SEVERAL PATHS by which traders brought their chattel to Natchez. Some sailed along the seaboard and the gulf to New Orleans. Some sailed down the Mississippi River. Most brought their slaves to Natchez by land, frequently along the Natchez Trace. The slaves would be assembled in coffles and led singly, in small groups or by the hundreds. The men, women and children were typically separated from each other, tied together by long chains or ropes. The caravan usually covered twenty to thirty miles a day and camped together at night, under the stars, covered by blankets that were collected by the drivers in the morning. Such a pace meant that the journey from Virginia to Natchez stretched into hellish months of chains, drudgery and depression. Many of the slaves even began looking forward to their arrival at the pens.

A view of the Natchez Trace today, by Carol Highsmith. *Library of Congress.*

Portrait of a Mississippi woman born "two years before the surrender," by Dorothea Lange. *Library of Congress.*

And then, they arrived at the pens.

William Wells Brown was a teenaged slave who was hired out by his master to work for a slave trader. Brown soon after escaped when his boat docked in Ohio. Shortly after, he wrote his autobiography, *Narrative of William W. Brown, a Fugitive Slave*, in which he described his experiences as an unwilling participant in the Mississippi River slave trade.

NATCHEZ MISSISSIPPI.

Natchez, Mississippi, by Henry Louis. *Beinecke Library at Yale University.*

When I learned the fact of my having been hired to a negro speculator, or a "soul driver," as they are generally called among slaves, no one can tell my emotions....

There was on the boat a large room on the lower deck, in which the slaves were kept, men and women, promiscuously—all chained two and two, and a strict watch kept that they did not get loose; a few cases have occurred in which slaves have got off their chains, and made their escape at landing-places, while the boats were taking in wood;—and with all our care, we lost one woman who had been taken from her husband and children, and having no desire to live without them, in the agony of her soul jumped overboard, and drowned herself.[119]

Brown ended his journey in New Orleans. He helped deposit the boat's cargo at a place that would have been similar to the Forks of the Road in Natchez:

Here the slaves were placed in a negro-pen, where those who wished to purchase could call and examine them. The negro-pen is a small yard, surrounded by buildings, from fifteen to twenty feet wide, with the exception of a large gate with iron bars. The slaves are kept in the building during the night, and turned out into the yard during the day. After the best of the stock was sold at a private sale at the pen, the balance were taken to the Exchange Coffee-House Auction Rooms kept by Isaac L. McCoy and sold at public auction.[120]

These overland routes were reminiscent of the earlier transatlantic Middle Passage. (Some of the early slaves might very well have both sailed across the Atlantic and later on been marched the thousand-mile journey from Richmond to Natchez.) Like those who endured the Middle Passage, the slaves sent in coffles to Natchez likewise would have understood that they were to never again see their loved ones—friends, parents, siblings, even children.[121]

DEPENDING ON YOUR PERSPECTIVE, the most awful among the myriad awful aspects of slavery might have been the separation of families. While some states forbade the practice of tearing children from their families, it is a matter of historical fact that such forced separations did occur, and with frequency.

Most slaves arrived in Natchez as singles from the age of thirteen to twenty-five. Buyers rarely bought family units or even husband-wife couples. Instead, the elderly and infants were left back where the march to Forks of the Road began—Maryland, Virginia and the Carolinas.[122]

More poignantly, there are records indicating the sale of parents away from their children and vice versa. The case of Lestitia Culberson is one among a plethora of examples. Culberson inherited a sickly seven-year-old boy named Tony. Seeing the boy wouldn't be much use on account of his frailty, she petitioned the courts to sell little Tony so that she could "purchase something else not liable to the same risk." The court approved and the sale was finalized.

Tony's mother, however, remained enslaved to Culberson.[123]

It wuz a big family of us. I think dare is 11 chillums. I don't know where none of them are at, if dey is living are [or] dead.
—*Silas Spotfore*

A grave marker in the slave cemetery at Mount Locust, by Carol Highsmith. *Library of Congress.*

Portrait of Annie Moore Schwein, born into slavery in Texas, by Dorothea Lange. *Library of Congress.*

Silas Spotfore woke up early, as always. As always, his mother was laying out the breakfast, and after hurriedly eating, she handed him a tin bucket filled with his dinner and gently pushed him in the direction of the fields.

Silas sleepily made his way to work. All he wanted was another hoecake and molasses. All he wanted was to be back on his mattress bed covered in corn husks. All he wanted was to be back with the old woman who, unable to do anything else, was assigned the task of watching the little folk. But he couldn't. Silas was old enough to go to work now. He was six years old.

Not allowed to go to school, not allowed to go to church, Silas still had an innate understanding of the world. He knew it was cold. His bare feet told him so. So did the trees bent under the weight of icicles. The cold made work miserable. But it also meant the approach of Christmas. And Silas eagerly awaited the holiday, when his mistress would give each slave a biscuit and an apple.

That evening, Silas returned to his shack, one day closer to Christmas. His grandmother was lying on the mattress. The area around her head was damp. So was her back. Silas quietly sat down to his meal. As always, he ate and went to bed. After all, tomorrow was another day—another long, monotonous, potentially painful day in the fields. A day of a slave.

But at least his kind masters gave him a biscuit and an apple every Christmas day.[124]

NATCHEZ BECAME AN AMERICAN byword for romance, adventure and wealth for three reasons: its beautiful and advantageous geography on the bluffs of the mighty Mississippi River; the backbone and tenacity of its residents; and slaves.[125]

In fact, Ronald Davis claims that slavery and cotton became the raison d'être for Natchez's existence:

> *The essential Natchez experience—possibly even more than the business of cotton—was the business of buying and selling slaves. Thousands of African-Americans were bought, sold, returned as "unfit" or diseased, sold again, swapped, mortgaged, inherited, traded, and handled as mere property on the auction blocks and in the slave-pens and warehouses of Natchez. The principal market sites stretched from Under-the-Hill, along Main Street, to the Forks just east of town. Courthouse steps and public parks, across the way from churches and school, hosted auctions whereupon black families were torn asunder in transactions that were the very underpinning of the*

district's life and economy. From the perspective of those African-Americans caught up in the trade, Natchez was little more than an incredibly horrible slave market.[126]

One of the greatest among many great tragedies of American slavery was the silencing of a people's history. The history is there, the bloodline is there, but the voice of nearly every slave has been suppressed.

Of course, some accounts of manumitted, escaped and later freed slaves exist (Frederick Douglas, Olaudah Equiano and William W. Brown, to name a few), yet the overwhelming majority of slaves were sold from their homelands to strangers, denied an education and forced to create a new community from scratch. (And that new community could be erased at the stroke of a pen.)

In the last two generations, historians have tried to restore the voice of the enslaved. Unfortunately, it is the voice of the historian more often than not extrapolating on "what it must have been like to be a slave"; "this slave felt this way, therefore his comrades must have felt the same"; "in an interview [decades later] the interviewee remembers a particular master thusly, therefore other slaves on the plantation must remember him the same." With limited resources, these historians have made a noble attempt to give a voice to the voiceless. ("Speak up for those who cannot speak for

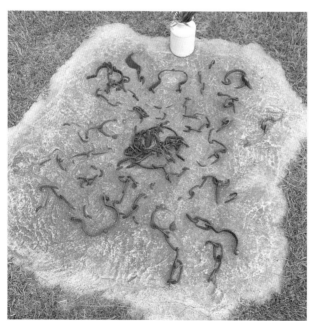

The Forks of the Road Memorial in Natchez. *Tayler Pomeroy/ Wikimedia Commons.*

themselves; ensure justice for those being crushed. Yes, speak up for the poor and helpless, and see that they get justice." Proverbs 31:8–9.)

However, the history of the enslaved as we learn it is more often than not the voice of collective "slaves," not the voice of "Frederick" or "William" or "Olaudah" or "Ibrahima" or the countless "X"s or those who couldn't even make a mark.

But that was the whole point of slavery—the exploitation of a people, the dehumanizing of a human, the commodification of a soul.

And yet, the former slaves of Natchez have always had a voice. It was a quiet voice at first, then a voice that grew and grew and grew in power.

It is a voice that was always there. It is part of the symphony of Natchez.

She was touched with a spiritual fire and permeated with a spiritual wholeness that had been forged in a crucible of suffering. She was, in that night, a spark of light that was neither of the earth nor September air, but eternal fire. Yet it was not that she stood there in pride for them to worship her or be in awe of her deep integrity. She was only a living sign and mark of all the best that any human being could hope to become. In her obvious capacity for love, redemptive and forgiving love, she was alive and standing on the highest peaks of her time and human personality. Peasant and slave, unlettered and untutored, she was nevertheless the best true example of the motherhood of her race, an ever present assurance that nothing could destroy a people whose sons had come from her loins. [127]
—Margaret Walker, Jubilee

CHAPTER 7

THE SAGA OF WILLIAM JOHNSON, THE BARBER OF NATCHEZ

He brought the lash down on her back. She screamed. He hit her again. And again. He had given his slave permission to attend church. Instead, she had "went off in some private Room, the Little Strumpet."[128] Eventually, satisfied that Lucinda had learned her lesson, her owner, William Johnson, sent her back to her slave husband.

As disappointed as he was in his female chattel, Johnson was beside himself in regard to another slave, Steven. Steven was a strong man and a capable worker. He was also an alcoholic. Despite it being illegal to sell liquor to slaves, Steven seemed to always have a ready supply. To make matters worse, he was a loud drunk, always getting into trouble when under the influence. His master, William Johnson, constantly bailed him out of jail and then whipped him.

March 19, 1838, proved a typical evening and following day for the troublesome slave: work, binge, hangover, run away, capture, beating. That evening, the slave master wrote in his diary:

> *Steven got drunk Last night and went of[f] and remained all night and was not Here this morning to go to Market.…He ran off 4 times in about three hours and Bill Nix Caught Him Every time, so He Brought Him Home after a while and I went to the stable and gave him a pretty sefveere thrashing with the cowhide—then he was perfectly Calm and Quite and could then do his work. Tis singular how much good it does some people to get whipped.*[129]

The William Johnson House in Natchez. *Ryan Starrett.*

Lucinda and Steven were not the only slaves of Johnson to be punished with the whip. In fact, the master reverted to scourging often enough that even the threat of a lashing inspired quick obedience.

> *I Caught old Mary to nite with a Basket with 7 or 8 unbaked Biscuit—I have reason to believe that she got them at the City Hotell, and the way I cursed her was the wright way and if Ever I can hear of her doing the Like again I will whip her until I make her faint.*[130]

William Johnson had invested a small fortune in his slaves, and he was determined to see that his property made good on his investment. And it all began with discipline.

THERE WAS TO BE a dance that night. But William Johnson, the wealthy, slave-owning barber of Natchez, would not be attending. Nor would any of his family or his apprentices. He had given strict orders for the latter to avoid the dance, but he could only hope they would obey him. Nothing good would ever come from attending those "darkey dances." One of businessman Johnson's greatest fears was that the color line would be blurred through miscegenation. It would be unforgiveable for a free man to mingle with inferiors.

There was to be another ball that same weekend. Many of Johnson's acquaintances and heroes would be attending. It promised to be a lavish affair to which all respectable Natchez residents would be invited. All, that is, except William Johnson.

The Natchez elite allowed their hair to be cut by the skilled barber. Many would even loiter around his shop, exchanging gossip and killing time. Some even had him over to their mansions and allowed him to cut and trim the hair of their children. A select few even visited him at his own impressive house at 210 State Street.

But they'd be damned if they allowed a Black man to attend one of their dances.

WILLIAM JOHNSON—ENTREPRENEUR, SUCCESSFUL BUSINESSMAN, respected resident, slave owner—lived as an outlier. He represented the most successful portion of a class on the fringe, neither slave nor citizen, but free person of color.

Natchez tended to look to New Orleans for cultural guidance. Whereas the bulk of Mississippi and the neighboring parishes of Louisiana embraced a much more conservative view of race relations, Natchez was laxer in its racial mores. Simply put, White men (especially rich White men) slept with Black women, and everyone knew it. Inevitably, offspring resulted. In Natchez, however, there was a strict sense of noblesse oblige, and a disproportionate number of concubines and their mixed children ended up being emancipated by their White lovers and fathers. By 1840, there were 283 free persons of color in Natchez's Adams County. (Five of these families, including Johnson's, owned anywhere from five to twenty slaves themselves.)

Despite the fortuitous events that allowed Johnson to live his life as a free man, it was, in many respects, an isolated existence. True, he had his family—wife, children and a sister and brother-in-law in New Orleans—and he ran a barbershop with all the concomitant gossip and joking and confiding, but his circle of intimates was severely limited. By his own choice, Johnson associated with Black slaves as little as possible. By the mandates of society, he associated with Whites on a strictly professional basis. Thus, Johnson could count the number of inner-circle friends on just one hand.

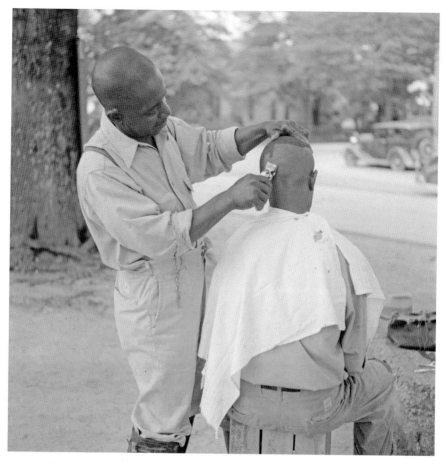

A Black Natchez barber cuts hair one hundred years after William Johnson practiced the same profession in the city. Photograph taken in 1940 by Marion Post Wolcott. *Library of Congress.*

Being a free Black barber, Johnson lived a professionally social but personally isolated life. Edwin Davis and William Hogan sum up the paradoxical life of the barber of Natchez:

> *William Johnson could attend none of these dances—not the "Grand Ball," nor the one marked by the presence of "Some Small Potatoes," nor the "Darkey Balls." He had little freedom of movement in social and entertainment circles, but there were few persons better informed about Natchez social and cultural happenings. That he was forced to satisfy this portion of his gregarious yearnings through the talk of his barbershop*

patrons may have become—although he never so stated—a spirit-corroding personal tragedy, for few of his contemporaries had more appetite for social intercourse. He could only listen and long as he shaved and clipped and anointed the heads of men preparing for the evening's hilarity. Later he could only scratch on a paper in the silence of his room as the pomaded ones danced.[131]

As socially isolated as Johnson was, there were plenty of moments that united the barber to his fellow Natchez residents. There is a basic common denominator in human persons that unites them in times of trial. Disease, disaster and death are egalitarian and must be faced by all persons, regardless of color. William Johnson, like his slaves and his condescending White counterparts, encountered these horsemen of the apocalypse.

THE DREADED FEVER WAS spreading. It was one of the few disadvantages to living in a prosperous commercial town. The riverboat traffic seemed to bring the plague every few years. Fortunately for the Johnson family, the patriarch was wealthy enough to escape the city. He prayed it wouldn't come to that.

Johnson's diary during September 1839 illustrates the rapid spread of yellow fever up and down the Mississippi River.

September

2   *Business dull—nothing new—Yellow fever Still very bad in New Orleans*

3   *Our town is very healthy at present and we Lern the Sickness is much worse in Orleans instead of a change for the better—God help them for I cannot.*

8   *Business good. Report Seys to night that there were 4 Deaths of Yellow Fever in Our Hospital to day.*

9   *Considerable Excitement about the Cases of Yellow Fever that occurred Yesterday at the Hospital and tis Said that there are ten or fifteen Cases of Sickness now at Different Places under the Hill.*

16   *There has been Considerable talk of Yellow Fever throughout the whole City to Day— 5 deaths*

17   *Several persons or Families has Left the City for the Country. I wrode out myself to the Quigless place to See how it would Suit to Live out thare in case of much Sickness in town....There were three Deaths in the City to Day.*

> 19   *No business a Doing of Any Account—All sorts of a run on the Rail Road Bank both to day and Yesterday for specie. The People are Leaving town very fast to Day for fear of Yellow Fever.*
>
> 22   *Business not very Good. People all Leaving the City very fast to Day. Mr. Coddingten Died this morning.*
>
> 23   *Citizens are Fast Leaving the City—I too made up my mind to Leave the City too.*[132]

The following day, William Johnson did, in fact, move his family to the country to escape the plague. His diary for September 25, 1839, states, "I am in the Country Sound as a Dollar."[133]

Johnson and his family would survive the yellow fever of 1839 and, surprisingly, every other frequent outbreak of the sickness as well. Many others in Natchez were not so lucky.

YELLOW FEVER AFFECTED MOST American cities, but Natchez, being a river town and in proximity to the frequent epicenter, New Orleans, experienced the epidemic often. The American Medical Association published a report in 1854 about the previous year's outbreak:

> *At Natchez, on the Mississippi River, three hundred miles above New Orleans, the epidemic commenced about the middle of July, and prevailed with unprecedented violence for more than two months….This city has maintained a quarantine against yellow fever ever since 1841; yet I have*

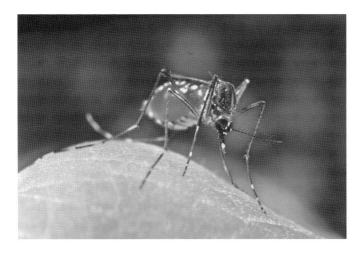

Aedes aegypti, a notorious vector of yellow fever in North America. *Centers for Disease Control and Prevention.*

been informed by some of the most respectable physicians of the place, that since that period scarcely a summer has passed without the appearance of some yellow fever cases there.[134]

The mysterious disease came on quickly, often beginning with a simple headache or fatigue, which progressed to fever, chills, nausea and vomiting. Sometimes called the "Black Vomit," a blackish mixture of blood and bile would be ejected by the victim.

Those who could often fled the city, and a strict quarantine isolated those who were affected. Nevertheless, yellow fever continued to be a yearly threat until the end of the nineteenth century.

In 1823, after the fever killed 312 Natchez residents, John A. Quitman wrote to his mother the following sober reminder of the fragile line between life and death in Natchez:

Three weeks since (in November) a severe frost banished the epidemic and we returned. It was painful to see the desolation of the streets. I looked in vain for faces with which I had been familiar. A gloom and sadness pervaded the whole place, and when friends met they pressed each other's hands in silence, or averted their faces and burst into tears.[135]

THE YEARS 1839 AND 1840 were particularly difficult for William Johnson. While his family was praying for deliverance from disease, destruction galloped into Natchez and nearly laid waste to the prosperous city on the bluff.

Just days after learning of an outbreak of yellow fever in New Orleans, Johnson heard the dreaded cry: "Fire!" He immediately leapt out of bed and rushed to do his civic duty on the fire line:

September
5 This Morning about 3 Oclock I was awakened by the Cry of Fire, Fire—I got up and ran with all possible Speed and found The Fire Burning on a stable up in Cotton Alley…it then spread Out in Different Dirrections and both Sids of the Ally was on fire at the same time—I comme[ce]ed to work on the Cotton that was in the shed With the help of others got it all out and at Least One half Burned up afterward.
6 Thank God I have wonce more Escaped, wonce more from Distruction[136]

An early photo of Natchez Under-the-Hill, taken in the later decades of the nineteenth century by Henry C. Norman. *New York Public Library.*

Johnson was, indeed, fortunate to have emerged from that fire unscathed. A four-block radius of Natchez's most prosperous business area was destroyed. He was not so lucky three weeks later, when another fire broke out.

> *It was near 9 Oclock to night that I saw from the Country a Large fire Given Light from Natchez and I mounted my horse and in a few minutes was in town and found, I am Sorry to say, One of the Larges Kinds of Fires on the Hill in State Street.*[137]

That fire (September 25, 1839) destroyed a house owned by Johnson's mother-in-law and managed by him. Fortunately for the barber, the house, which cost $3,000 to build, was insured up to $2,000, and the insurance

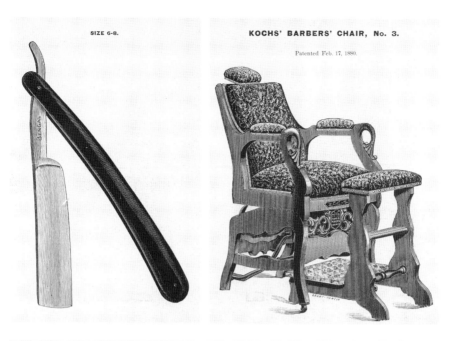

This page: Items from the 1884 Chicago-based Theo A. Kochs Barbers' Supplies catalog. *Internet Archive*.

company paid out the full amount to Johnson. When he returned home after the yellow fever scare, he immediately set about rebuilding the house.[138]

Johnson was fortunate enough to escape most of the damage the frequent fires of Natchez caused and wealthy enough to rebuild when he wasn't. One hundred years later, many Natchez residents were not so lucky when one of the worst fires in U.S. history killed 209 revelers at a famous Natchez nightclub.

As FREQUENT AND DEADLY as fires could be, Natchez's greatest natural disaster came from the skies. On May 7, 1840, the second-deadliest tornado in U.S. history struck Natchez, killing 317 people. William Johnson recorded: "[May] 7 To Day was in the aforenoon very pleasant Day until past One Oclock and then we had rain, with One of the Greatest Tornadoes that Ever was Seen in this place before."[139]

That afternoon, the residents of Natchez saw large, ominous black clouds to the south. Some seemed stationary, while other dark clouds began whirling northward, underneath the darkening sky. At two o'clock in the afternoon, the dinner bells in the large hotels began to ring. Those who could rushed inside. Darkness enveloped the land. Many people lit candles and prayed that the storm would quickly pass. It didn't. The next day, the *Natchez Free Trader* reported:

> *A few moments afterwards, the rain was precipitated in tremendous cataracts rather than in drops. In another moment the tornado, in all its wrath was upon us. The strongest buildings shook as if tossed with an earthquake; the air was black with whirling eddies of house walls, roofs, chimnies, huge timbers torn from distant ruins, all shot through the air as if thrown from a mighty catapult.*[140]

Minutes later, Natchez was in ruins. Although the storm hung in the air for half an hour, the tornado itself swept through the city on the bluffs and did all its damage in only three to five minutes. It only needed a few minutes to become one of the deadliest tornadoes in U.S. history.

> *For about five minutes it was more like the explosive force of gunpowder than any thing else it could have been compared to. Hundreds of rooms were burst open as sudden as if barrels of gunpowder had been ignited in each.*[141]

The tornado had landed about a mile below the city, near the plantation home known as Bellevue. It destroyed the mansion and the ancient forest in which it stood and then headed north. With a two-mile front, it hit Vidalia and Natchez and everything in between.

> *At the Natchez Landing on the river the ruin of dwellings, stores, steamboats, flat boats, was almost entire from the Vidalia ferry to the Mississippi Cotton Press. A few torn fragments of dwellings still remain, but they can scarcely be called shelters.*
>
> *In the upper city, or Natchez on the hill, scarcely a house escaped damage or utter ruin.*[142]

Fortunately for neighboring Vidalia, only one person was killed. Judge Keeton was killed while eating dinner at a friend's house. Natchez was not so lucky.

Of the fifty or sixty flatboats docked outside the city, only six survived the tornado. It was estimated that about two hundred flatboatmen were drowned in the river. The Steamboat Hotel became the graveyard of at least nine occupants. One, Mrs. Alexander, was dug out and taken to the hospital in critical condition. Her two children were found in her arms, dead.

The day after the tornado, about fifty Natchez residents were buried. Over the course of the next several days, many more would die of wounds and join their companions in the ground. Many (like the drowned flatboatmen) would never be found. A columnist for the *Natchez Free Trader* summed up the situation:

> *Meanwhile we beg the indulgence of our kind friends and patrons for a few days, in which time we shall be able to get our office in some order. The Free Trader office building has been crushed in and much shattered. We are all in confusion, and surrounded by the destitute, the houseless, the wounded and the dying. Our beautiful city is shattered as if it had been stormed by all the cannon of Austerlitz. We are peeled and desolate.*[143]

Johnson wrote: "[May] 8 Several persons found during this Day that was Killed under the Houses Oh what times, no One Ever seen such times."[144] A week later, he recorded yet more destruction: [May] 17 I took my Horse together with Sterns and Jno Jackomine and went into the Swamp—We found the road in a terrible condition Indeed—trees was a Lying all over the Road in Every Direction—Maj Jno Winns Plantation Houses were all

Natchez-Under-the-Hill, painted in the mid-nineteenth century by Frederick Hawkins Piercy. *Internet Archive.*

Blown over—Gin and all—and the water from the River was very high and running over for an Hundred yards or more."[145]

In addition to the 317 deceased, the town suffered an estimated $5 million in damages.[146] But, as they had been doing for over a century, the residents of Natchez rolled up their sleeves and began rebuilding their beautiful city on the bluff.

PERIODICALLY, DISEASE, DISASTER AND destruction affected all the residents of Natchez. William Johnson was no exception. He, too, like his Black slaves, his White "superiors" and his fellow freedmen, dreaded sickness and natural disasters. Otherwise, life was good. True, he lived the life of an outlier, fitting in with neither the caste below nor the caste above. But there were plenty of amenities that helped assuage the loneliness he must have felt.

In the first place, there was his family. Johnson was close to his sister Adelia and her husband and fellow barber, James Miller, in New Orleans, and made frequent trips downriver to the Crescent City to visit them. More important, he had his wife, Ann. Ann had given her husband eleven children, all of whom became a source of intense pride for their father.

He fed them well, made sure they had sturdy clothes, gave them small allowances and did not hesitate to call a doctor when one fell ill. (He lived in an era when a doctor was most often called as a last resort, due to their expense. Home remedies were the norm. Yet, William Johnson took no chances with his children's health.)

Johnson loved his children. He loved to be in their presence and play with them. He enjoyed taking walks with them, eating blueberries, playing marbles, sports and racing little sailboats with them.[147] But, more important, he wanted to ensure that they had a good start in life.

But perhaps Johnson's greatest gift to his children was the education he gave them—both book learning and practical education. It must have been incredibly difficult (and heart-wrenching) for this strong and successful Black man to educate his Black children in the South in the mid-nineteenth century. He knew who his children were—freedmen—but what could they become? Citizens? Official community leaders? The social equal of a White person? No, no and no. They would always be colored. They would always be reminded that they were inferior. And yet, Johnson surely knew his own personal worth. He was determined that his children understood theirs as well.

William Johnson was determined to attempt the herculean task of making his children self-actualize as strong and dignified colored persons in a society set up to keep such persons subservient. And he would do so through education.

Being adamant that his children be able to compete and succeed in school, Johnson took pains to teach each to read and write before he enrolled them in school. He closely followed their progress, rewarding them when they flourished and using his hard hand of discipline when they underachieved.

Johnson was rewarded for his patience, perseverance and love. All eleven of his children not only survived in an era of high infant mortality but also grew into freedmen and women themselves, eventually experiencing the citizenship their father always longed for.

ON MONDAY, JUNE 16, 1851, William Johnson decided to check on his farm about seven miles south of Natchez. He brought along with him his son, one of his mulatto apprentices and a slave.

Johnson had been having problems with Baylor Wynn, one of his neighbors, regarding the boundary between their two properties. Wynn was one of the few thorns in Johnson's side, but even that situation had been cleared up when the courts ruled in favor of Johnson (who, in turn, for the sake of peace, willingly lowered the amount he was to receive from the settlement). Otherwise, his life was going along remarkably well (especially considering what he might have been had he not been emancipated). He had his barbershops, his brick homes in town, a handful of investments, racing horses, a bathhouse, his farmlands and his slaves—thirty throughout his life.[148] William Johnson was a man of consequence—albeit a noncitizen of an "inferior" race, but respected, propertied, monied and comfortable nonetheless.

Life was good for the forty-two-year-old barber of Natchez as he rode back home that Monday evening with his son, his employee and his slave, smoking a cigar. The *Natchez Daily Courier* soon after reported:

> *Our city was very much excited on Tuesday morning, by hearing that what could only be deemed a horrible and deliberate murder had been committed upon an excellent and inoffensive man. It was ascertained that William Johnson, a free man of color, born and raised in Natchez, and holding a respected position on account of his character, intelligence and deportment, had been shot, together with a young mulatto boy, about three miles below town, as they were returning home just before sunset on Monday evening last, in company with a son of Johnson and one of his negro slaves.*[149]

In a city known for violence, fights and dueling, William Johnson, a freedman of color who frequently interacted financially with Whites and sometimes even took them to court, had never been beaten or attacked and had never been in a fight or a duel. He had never been the victim of any violent act. But on a warm summer day in 1851, he was laid in the ground with three exit wounds in his lung, stomach and arm.

THE TRIAL OF BAYLOR Wynn for the murder of William Johnson captivated Natchez residents for two years. On June 21, 1851, the *Mississippi Free Trader* reported:

> *The Examination of Baylor Winn for the shooting of William Johnson, will take place in the Court House this morning, and will doubtless attract general attention. The most eloquent and talented gentlemen of the Natchez bar have been engaged, both for the prosecution and the defense.*

> *So great an interest has been excited in our community by this tragical occurrence, we shall report the evidence given to-day verbatim, for the information of our patrons in our next paper.*

Like Johnson, Baylor Wynn was also of mixed blood. Unlike Johnson, he was able to "pass" as White. There were always suspicions, but he was able to convince his fellow citizens that he was a mix of White and Indian rather than White and Black. The former mixture made him legally "White"; the latter made him an "inferior," a noncitizen.

Because the witnesses were Black and mulatto, they could not testify in court. Baylor Wynn went home a free man.[150]

William Johnson never got posthumous justice. Perhaps as a consolation, the Natchez community allowed the barber to be buried in the White cemetery.[151] That honor did little good for his mixed-race children, who were forced to spend the next dozen years as noncitizens, stuck, like their father, between two worlds—and then the rest of their lives as second-class Americans.

BIOGRAPHERS EDWIN DAVIS AND William Hogan neatly sum up the worldview of the enigmatic "Barber of Natchez":

> *If William Johnson heard the Southern phrase "poor white trash," he understood and appreciated its meaning and the tone of contemptuous derision with which it was uttered. As a businessman who enjoyed material substance and community standing in a trade catering to whites, he avoided intimacy both with what he regarded as poor white trash and with poor black trash. As an individual who endeavored to pattern his conduct according to his conception of the code of white gentlemen, he avoided close association with inferior persons of any estate or complexion. Class and caste existed then, as now, among Southern Negroes, and the barber carefully maintained his position at the top of his personal social and economic heap.[152]*

William Johnson was a self-made man. He rose from slavery to become one of the most successful businessmen in Natchez. He is the embodiment of the American Dream, of rags to riches. He was a good citizen (with neither the official designation nor the rights of a citizen), a devoted husband and father and an exemplar of ambition, drive and industry. He bettered himself, his family and his community.

But he became such a success on the backs of his human property, the very system in which his mother and maternal grandparents toiled under, and the system in which he himself might very well have lived out his life. Rather than working the fields and bearing the lash himself, he put others to work, sometimes motivating them with the whip, and used their profits to give himself a good life.

Chapter 8

Black Soldier of the Republic

1864

On the afternoon of Sunday, February 7, the citizens of Natchez took to the bluffs of the city. For two days, word had spread that a large Confederate army was advancing from the west. Now, the rumors were proven true. At 2:00 p.m., the spectators watched as a line of one thousand Confederate infantry and cavalry emerged from the woods outside Vidalia, Louisiana. The troops waved battle flags and moved in a line toward the village—and to Natchez, beyond. Another five hundred Confederates waited in reserve. Natchez had been under Union control for nearly two years. The spectators hoped that day to see "their brave boys drive the Yankees and niggers into the river." Their cheers must have carried far over the water.[153]

From their high vantage points, the spectators also saw that the Union forces stationed at Vidalia had done what they could to prepare for the Confederate advance. The Union soldiers there, who numbered perhaps 150, had erected a breastwork of cotton bales across the road leading into town. They had positioned men behind a ditch that crossed the battlefield. They had stationed men at the sides of the town, near the river, to prevent flanking. They had acquired a twelve-pound howitzer that could fire exploding shells. Three gunboats and an armed tugboat floated in the Mississippi River behind them, preparing to fire on the Confederates from the water.[154]

As soon as the Confederate line emerged from the woods, some two miles distant from Vidalia, the commanding Union officer there, Colonel B.G. Farrar, sent word to the main Union forces at Natchez: send help, and send it now.

At Natchez, Lieutenant Colonel Hubert A. McCaleb received the call for reinforcements and began rounding up most of the men under his command and directing them to Natchez Under-the-Hill. Though McCaleb himself was a battle-hardened veteran, the 432 men at his command had never taken part in a battle. Most had been soldiers for only a few weeks. At the start of the Civil War, they had been enslaved. McCaleb's men were the Second Mississippi Heavy Artillery, African Descent. Abraham Lincoln's Emancipation Proclamation had made it possible for them to join the Union army. They were illiterate and untrained but would soon be tempered by the fire of battle.

In all, McCaleb directed 432 men as they climbed into the steamship *Diligent*, moored at the Under-the-Hill landing. With the men aboard, a bell was rung and the ropes holding the *Diligent* to the shore were loosed. Across the river, McCaleb mounted a large gray horse and formed his men into a battle line. He was an imposing man at six feet, two inches tall and weighing nearly three hundred pounds. He had fought in numerous Civil War battles to that point, including at Fort Gibson, Meridian and Vicksburg.[155] McCaleb's men took their position on the road in front of the town. When the Confederates reached Vidalia, they would first clash with McCaleb's Black soldiers.[156]

The Confederate force that day was made up of soldiers from Texas and Louisiana and led by a French nobleman named Prince Camille Armand Jules Marie de Polignac. His soldiers, unable to pronounce his name, called him simply "Polecat." Polignac hoped at the least to clear the countryside of Union cotton planters; capture horses, mules and cows; and provide an opportunity for the Union garrison at Vidalia to desert. At best, he hoped to capture Vidalia and from there to immediately attack Natchez.[157]

Polignac led his men toward Vidalia in "gallant style," as "ACE," a witness in Natchez, described it. At the front of the Confederate line waved three battle flags. As the Confederates came within range, the Union defenders fired their howitzer, and the gunboats floating in the Mississippi opened fire. The guns' exploding shells reached the Confederate line, sending the men back into the "friendly timber" they had emerged from. The howitzer was a deterrent, but its carriage soon broke, rendering it useless. The Confederates, who had maintained an advance group of skirmishers throughout the engagement, realized that the gun was no longer functional and began again

Left: Abraham Lincoln, circa 1864, by William Willard. *National Portrait Gallery, Smithsonian Institution*.

Below: "Charge of the Phalanx," from *The Black Phalanx* (1888). *Internet Archive*.

to advance in a line. They "seemed to expect an easy victory," the witness wrote.

But the initial barrage of artillery had given McCaleb and his Black soldiers time to arrive on the battlefield and begin to take their defensive positions. McCaleb on his large horse was "a mark for all the enemy's sharpshooters," but he continued to maneuver his men to a defensible hill in front of the town, the Confederate skirmishers firing all the way.

Camille Armand Jules Marie, Prince de Polignac. *Internet Archive.*

"By the time I had reached this point the enemy's skirmishers had advanced near enough to become very annoying," McCaleb wrote after the battle, "and although my men had never before been under fire, they came up promptly on the double-quick, and formed a line under a heavy skirmish fire, with as much coolness as could veterans of many battles."[158]

The Black men yelled as they took their positions. When the main Confederate line had come within 150 yards of McCaleb's men, McCaleb ordered the men to fire.

"They executed it by giving one splendid volley, well aimed," McCaleb wrote. "I immediately ordered the men to load, which they did with great coolness, and with one more well-aimed volley, the rebel ranks were broken, and their men, panic-stricken, ran away in great confusion."

Polignac's hopes of capturing Vidalia broke along with the Confederate ranks, and the men retreated ten miles into the Louisiana interior. The Confederates lost six men, had another ten wounded and had eight captured. No Union soldier was killed or wounded.[159]

Colonel Bernard Gaines Farrar Jr., the overall Union commander at Vidalia that day, was lauded for his decisive victory over a force that outnumbered his three to one. The gunboats in the Mississippi had played an important support role. But it was McCaleb's Black soldiers who had fired the close-range volleys that broke the Confederate army.

"Veterans could not have behaved better," the witness in Natchez wrote. The engagement was the first of several actions the Second Mississippi Heavy Artillery would see in the final years of the Civil War. The soldiers would defend Natchez for the remainder of the war and venture into the surrounding countryside to engage the Confederates eight more times before the war's end. Of the four Black regiments stationed at Natchez during the war, they saw by far the most action.[160]

HISTORIAN JUSTIN BEHREND DESCRIBED Natchez in the years before the Civil War this way: "The Natchez District was a region of vast cotton plantations and slaveholdings…[with] a large African American population majority, some of the richest cotton land in the South, and a vast rural hinterland connected by the centrally located city of Natchez."[161]

The demographic imbalance of the district was such that Whites were outnumbered many times over; Black slaves made up 82 percent of the population in 1860. Even before war broke out, news of John Brown's raid at Harpers Ferry stoked in Natchez slaves a feeling of "uneasiness" and in Natchez planters the fear of a large-scale rebellion.

After the war started, but before Natchez had been captured and occupied by Union troops, the Black residents of the district lived in a hell worse than that of the antebellum days. They were as eager to hear word of advancing Union troops—and tidings of emancipation—as White Natchez citizens were paranoid that war would bring with it a widespread slave insurrection.

With the outbreak of war, many White men left Natchez to fight in Virginia, increasing the demographic imbalance—and the paranoia of a slave revolt. White men left behind resorted to draconian tactics to put down any chance of rebellion, torturing and executing many slaves suspected of harboring feelings of dissension. At least 50 slaves—and as many as 209—were executed.[162]

During the first years of the war, before the occupation of Natchez, enslaved men were overheard on plantations talking about Lincoln, emancipation and advancing Union troops. Sometimes, they expressed the desire to join the Union army and "stand up like men," as one enslaved man put it. The fact that these sentiments were recorded sadly implies that in many cases slaves were severely punished for expressing them.[163]

Vicksburg fell on July 4, 1863, and two weeks later, Union troops occupied Natchez (which had surrendered the year before). The Federal presence at Natchez made the city a mecca for Black people from all over the region, many of whom had been living a life of flight and subsistence in the Mississippi and Louisiana countrysides for a year already.

Natchez from 1863 to 1865 was a fortified and unassailable Union stronghold, and the Black flight to the city is one of the reasons why. Five thousand Union troops were barracked at Natchez in those years, and of those, more than three thousand were Black. Natchez's Black soldiers had been recruited from the refugee camps and plantations in and around Natchez. When a Black male refugee appeared in Natchez, he was given a choice of three occupations by Federal authorities: work on building

"Contrabands Coming into Camp in Consequence of the Proclamation." Originally published in *Harper's Weekly*, 1863. *Smithsonian Libraries*.

fortifications in the city, work on abandoned plantations outside the city or enlist in the Union army.

As Union soldiers, the men found themselves less well equipped, prepared and provisioned than their White counterparts elsewhere in the country. Many had been enslaved together on the same plantations before the war. They did not know how to be soldiers. Nevertheless, they set about drilling, building, cleaning and obeying the strict rules of camp life. They had inadequate clothing, shoes, food and weapons. They used the lawns of private homes, the town squares and the bluffs above the city as their training grounds. They ranged into the countryside hunting vegetables and meat. They found themselves barracked at Under-the-Hill, on the bluffs above the city and at Forks of the Road, the old slave market where some may well have been sold.

Union officers tried to enforce discipline among Natchez's Black soldiers. Orders issued in 1863 demonstrate the problems that came with enlisting thousands of formerly enslaved men. Women and children—the families of the soldiers—were visiting camp when they weren't supposed to. Men were "committing nuisances" in improper places—a euphemism for defecation and urination. Guns were being fired off in camp at random times. Whiskey had to be rationed in the strictest and most measured ways. The men had families scattered in the various refugee camps around Natchez, and they tried their hardest to see them—even when that meant leaving their encampments without permission.

Despite officers' efforts to bring cleanliness and order to the camps of Black soldiers, disease ran rampant, killing an incredible number. About one in three Black soldiers stationed in Natchez during the war died of disease, a ratio far greater than that of the Union army in general (about one in thirteen). Smallpox, malaria, measles and general filth in the camps were the deadly culprits. The miserable conditions of life in Natchez combined to drive up desertion in the army. At some point in the war, 13 percent of the Black soldiers at Natchez went AWOL.[164]

IN THE WINTER OF 1863, Polignac and his Confederates found themselves able to move freely in the Louisiana hinterland, able to strike at Vidalia and Natchez at will, and able to take advantage of a Union force of untrained and untested Black soldiers. But Colonel B.G. Farrar, who would rebuff their

A "Negro" Regiment in Action, by Thomas Nast. Originally published in *Harper's Weekly*, 1863. *Metropolitan Museum of Art*.

attack on Vidalia in the coming weeks, was not afraid to venture deep into the Louisiana countryside to strike at the Confederates where they felt most comfortable. And the men he relied on for one such strike were the Second Mississippi Heavy Artillery.

Farrar was an educated St. Louis native who had already fought in major Civil War battles—the Battle of Wilson's Creek in Missouri and the Siege of Vicksburg under Ulysses S. Grant—by the time he reached Natchez. He would eventually assume overall command of both Natchez and Vidalia. In 1863, he commanded at Vidalia and proved himself to be a tenacious defender, unafraid to strike at Confederates in Louisiana when the opportunity presented itself.[165]

One such opportunity arose in early December 1863. With Christmas approaching, word reached Farrar via a local, unnamed woman that Confederate leadership in Louisiana was planning a military ball at Johnson's Plantation, a home on the Black River, thirty-three miles from Natchez. Farrar immediately realized the opportunity: he could strike the ball in the middle of the night. The Confederates there would be caught completely off guard. They would be relaxed, unprepared to resist, drunk and gathered together. Farrar could capture the whole lot if he acted decisively and had enough men.

Farrar's problem was twofold. First, the ball would begin in just a few hours. There was little time to prepare, and he would need to leave immediately to reach the ball by horseback that night. Second, he did not have enough men. His cavalry would have been an ideal force to carry out the mission, but they were on the Natchez side of the river, scouting against a possible Confederate attack from Wirt Adams, who had recently marched within seven miles of the city with a large force.

Farrar thought quickly and hatched an audacious plan that could have gone wrong in one hundred ways. He procured several dozen horses and formed a new, makeshift cavalry unit from the men who happened to be stationed at Vidalia at that moment. His new unit was made up of ten soldiers of the Missouri Thirtieth Infantry, nicknamed the "Shamrock Regiment" because of its makeup of mostly Irishmen, and twenty-five soldiers of the Second Mississippi Heavy Artillery, African Descent, as yet untested by battle. By 8:00 p.m. that night, Farrar was leading the new cavalrymen himself through the swamps between Vidalia and Johnson's Plantation. The route was partially submerged, and the group moved slowly, riding through the night. But they made incremental progress and by 4:00 a.m. had approached to within a half mile of the plantation, unnoticed and ready to surprise the Confederates. "The brilliant lights which gleamed from the windows and the sweet cadence of the music told that all went merry within," a newspaper would report.

Farrar directed his force to surround the plantation. Then, he crept to the front doors of the house. He unholstered his pistol and, backed by a group of Black soldiers of the Second Mississippi Heavy Artillery, "dashed" into the ballroom. Inside, he announced to what must have been a flabbergasted party that he expected every Confederate officer and soldier inside to surrender. The Confederates offered no resistance.

Having achieved victory, and apparently feeling quite secure in that victory, Farrar then told the partygoers that they should continue with the festivities. He directed the band to continue playing, took the hand of a young Southern woman and led her onto the dance floor, where they began to waltz. Farrar's display must have added salt to the wounds of the captured Confederates, who looked on as prisoners of Black Mississippians.

As the sun began to rise, Farrar and his men marched the Confederates outside to their own mounts. Saying their goodbyes to the distraught women and friends they had been reveling with just a couple hours before, the Confederates rode away, each guarded by a Union soldier. It took Farrar and his men several hours to arrive back in Vidalia, but they had returned

"Phalanx Cavalry Bringing in Confederate Prisoners," from *The Black Phalanx* (1888). *Internet Archive*.

by 11:00 a.m. The group had covered sixty-six miles and had pulled off the mission from start to finish in fifteen hours. From Vidalia, the Confederate prisoners were ferried across the river to Natchez, where Farrar made it a point to march them through the streets, accompanied by twelve soldiers of the Second Mississippi Heavy Artillery. While marching, the Confederates protested: "Can't we have a white guard, colonel?" one asked. "No," Farrar replied. "The negroes took you and it is right that they should guard you."[166]

Colonel B.G. Farrar. *Internet Archive.*

Though life as a soldier in the Union army proved in many ways to be a miserable existence for Black soldiers at Natchez, their story was also, as historian Ronald L.F. Davis put it, "an uplifting tale of courage, valor, fortitude, and risk-taking."

The story of Farrar's raid on the ball is an example of courageous and capable action on the part of Natchez's Black soldiers. And Farrar's conspicuous parade of the prisoners through Natchez's streets was a message to the city's citizens, many of whom were still supporters of the Confederacy.

The more than three thousand Black soldiers encamped at Natchez during the war ultimately ensured that even though large Confederate forces moved in the vicinity of the city on all sides, Natchez was never truly threatened with recapture. They fought on the battlefield when Confederates neared but also worked on building the sprawling Fort McPherson in the northwest part of Natchez and ventured into the countryside around Natchez in projections of Union power.[167]

THE BEHAVIOR OF BLACK soldiers in Natchez showed that, as one reporter visiting their encampments put it, they are "ready to fight for their own liberty, and the safety of our common country."[168]

CHAPTER 9

FAULKNER TOLD THE TRUTH

Dick Dana and Octavia Dockery, Beneficiaries of the "Lost Cause"

Dick Dana and Octavia Dockery took the stage in Jackson, Mississippi's auditorium. The crowds waited in hushed anticipation. Dick Dana, the quintessential southern gentleman, sat on the stage and showed the audience why he was known as "the maestro of Natchez." His skill at the piano moved the crowd to tears. "From the first moment Dana, with the manner and poise of one born to his art, touched the keys of the piano, the audience seemed to sense that they were hearing notes that came from the soul of a man to whom music was something more than love, something more than life, something more than human passion."

After Dana awed the crowds with his melodies and voice, his friend of nearly thirty years took the stage. Miss Octavia Dockery was "the colorful companion of his solitudes…[and] mistress of the mansion that so long closed them in from the world in which they once played distinguished parts."

Octavia regaled the audience with tales of her youth. The daughter of a Confederate general, a published writer and the current mistress of what was now one of America's most famous antebellum mansions, she had a natural gift of gab and the charm of an aging but still vivacious southern belle.

The two, Dana and Dockery, were perfect representatives of the South—at least a certain segment of the South. They were the progeny of a bygone era, of fallen families and of lost dreams. They were the ultimate could-have-beens, the face of nostalgia, the Lost Cause personified. They had their audience completely smitten. So enthralled was the crowd, in fact, that the pair was planning to offer the same performance throughout the major cities of the South.[169]

An unidentified Confederate soldier and his presumed wife, taken sometime between 1861 and 1865. *Library of Congress.*

Dick Dana was a gentleman of bona fide Southern stock. He was charming, educated and pedigreed. He even dressed the part in a "frock coat, a slouch hat and a string tie...to take on the appearance of a professional Southerner....[He] sported a 'Buffalo Bill' mustache and goatee." So proper and nostalgic did he look that the residents of Natchez took to calling him "Colonel Dana."[170]

The military title brought back memories of his illustrious Confederate ancestry. His father was Reverend Charles Backus Dana, the highly respected rector of Trinity Episcopal Church in Natchez. More important, Reverend Dana had been Robert E. Lee's minister back at Christ Church in Alexandria, Virginia.

After steering his Natchez flock through the devastation of the Civil War, the reverend gradually began to put the pieces of his shattered world back together. Soon, his church membership, coffers and family began to grow. He bought a large home named Glenwood and welcomed his second son, Richard "Dick" Dana, in 1871.

Two years later, Reverend Dana died at sixty-seven. When his oldest son, Charles, died during the Spanish-American War in 1898, Dick Dana became the sole inheritor of Glenwood. His name and his inheritance, coupled with his education at the Chamberlain-Hunt boarding school in Port Gibson and at Vanderbilt University (not to mention his musical talents), inevitably

Natchez Hotel, Natchez, Mississippi. *Lucius Marion Lampton, MD Historical Images Collection. Mississippi State University Libraries.*

made Dick Dana the face of the New South—the New South that would never forget the Old South.

Octavia Dockery, too, was of impeccable southern stock, perhaps even more so than Dick Dana. Octavia's father was Thomas Dockery—rather, General Thomas Dockery. Confederate General Thomas Dockery.

General Dockery commanded a brigade of CSA troops from Arkansas, fought at the battle of Port Gibson, was captured by Federal troops at Vicksburg, promptly violated his parole and fought bravely for the doomed Confederacy until its surrender in 1865. Afterward, he was ruined—financially and personally. He lost his land, his slaves and, for a while, his family.

In an attempt to rebuild what he had lost, General Dockery took a job in Houston and left his wife and two daughters with an uncle in his wife's native Coahoma County. When his wife died in 1880, the widower-general moved with his daughters to New York. It did not take long for the embittered Dockery to entirely unravel. Unable to provide for his children, Dockery married his elder daughter off to a fifty-five-year-old friend who, in 1896, moved his young, new wife and her sister, Octavia, to Natchez. General Thomas Dockery, hero of the Confederacy, died penniless in a New York boardinghouse two years later.

The White South never forgot General Dockery's sacrifices.[171]

DICK DANA AND OCTAVIA Dockery, gentleman and southern belle, concert pianist and published writer, lived together in Dana's inherited estate, Glenwood. Octavia's aged brother-in-law had moved his wife and her sister into Glenwood in 1911. Within a year, both he and his wife were dead, leaving Octavia alone in the world. Yet, in an act of selfless gallantry, Dana promised the dying sister that he would continue to look after the forty-seven-year-old orphaned Octavia. She continued to live at Glenwood.

The two genteel artist-friends, scions of the romantic Old South, now alone in the world, turned their attention to making their antebellum estate prosperous. All they had was their land, their home and each other.[172]

DICK DANA'S FATHER HAD purchased Glenwood and its accompanying forty-five acres in 1866. It was a large estate, built in 1841 on the outskirts of Natchez with two and a half stories, four chimneys, a large veranda and an idyllic, southern balcony.

Oldest House in Mississippi, "Kings Tavern" Natchez, Mississippi. *Lucius Marion Lampton, MD Historical Images Collection. Mississippi State University Libraries.*

The estate itself contained plenty of land for chickens, hogs and goats, as well as ample woods in which to wander. True to her southern roots, Octavia added to the charm by planting a garden.

Glenwood became so distinct, so exceptional that, in the twilight of her [its] life, tourists from all over the country began flocking to Natchez in order to visit the famous Glenwood estate.[173]

IN 1931, ONE OF Natchez's most eccentric and talented citizens—"a visionary with a steel-vise mind"[174]—began to promote an idea that would help revitalize an economically crumbling city.

It was said that Katherine Grafton Miller had fifteen ideas a minute, "thirteen of them ridiculous, two brilliant or something close to it."[175] Undoubtedly her most brilliant idea (not to mention her determination to see it through) was to create the Natchez Pilgrimage.

Miller, the president of the Natchez Garden Club, decided it was time for a party—a large party. She decided to invite the nation—in the midst of the Great Depression—to Natchez to make a pilgrimage to its opulent mansions. The city would charge admission and use the money to restore the antebellum homes. Despite local skepticism and prognostications of doom, Miller enforced her will. As a result, thousands flocked to Natchez and poured desperately needed cash into the city. Six and a half decades after its ruinous rebellion, Natchez was once again an exemplar of "the good ole days." Almost a century later, the Pilgrimage has expanded into a five-week spring and fall festival and is still one of the city's major industries.

The Pilgrimage began at precisely the time that one of Natchez's famous abodes was garnering national attention in its own right. Natchez historian Harnett Thomas Kane noted: "For a time Natchez had even a third pilgrimage....Dick Dana was inviting the world to come to [Glenwood], where another part of the New South lived."[176]

As the sun began to set on August 4, 1932, sixty-one-year-old Dick Dana and sixty-eight-year-old Octavia Dockery stood outside their neighbor's house. Jennie Merrill had been a thorn in their sides. The ornery recluse had called the police time and time again, complaining of her Glenwood neighbors. She had filed lawsuit after lawsuit seeking reparations for damaged property. Evidently, Dana and Octavia's ranching enterprise had interfered with Merrill's gardening interests. The formers' goats had repeatedly entered Merrill's Glenburnie estate and helped themselves to her vegetation and flowers. And Merrill, a daughter of the Old South and a member of the Natchez aristocracy herself, expected compensation. Only, she refused to confront her rival-neighbors in person. That would have been beneath her dignity. After all, her family was much more established in Natchez than either the Danas (who came to Natchez via Virginia in 1841) or the Dockerys (who arrived from New York via Arkansas in 1896). And Jennie Merrill wasn't just landed. She was rich. Very rich.

George Pearls, Edgar Allen Poe Newell and Emily Burns, three Black persons from Natchez, soon joined Dick and Octavia outside Merrill's home. The five stood outside Glenburnie, in the heart of the Jim Crow South, with one common goal.[177]

Shortly after, the unlikely conspirators were squatting beneath Merrill's house, listening intently in an attempt to locate the old recluse. George Pearls crawled from beneath the porch, covered his face and silently walked up the steps and inside the house.[178]

The four accomplices heard a scream, a thud and then the loud crack of a pistol, followed by two more cracks in rapid succession, and then another thud as something heavy crashed to the floor.

Dick and Octavia ran inside and surveyed the scene. Merrill herself lay in her bedroom bleeding to death. There was a bullet in the wall of the dining

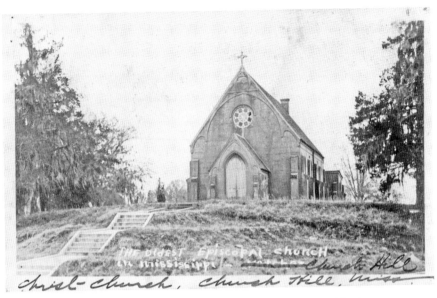

Christ Church. *Charles Johnson Faulk Collection. Mississippi State University Libraries.*

room, where the scuffle had taken place, and a trail of blood leading to her room to which she had tried to escape. And then there was the growing pool of blood beneath her.

The blood trail would soon expand as the men moved quickly to hide their crime. There could be no doubt that a number of Black workers near Merrill's estate heard the gunshots. In addition, her closest friend, Duncan Minor, would soon arrive for his customary evening visit. It was imperative to dispose of the body.

But before that, they needed to ransack the house, which was, after all, the whole reason for their nocturnal visit to Glenburnie.[179]

DICK AND OCTAVIA NEEDED money badly. Their mansion—Dana's inheritance—was in a state of foreclosure. Actually, it had been for two decades. Using one legal trick after another, Octavia had managed to keep the status of the Glenwood estate in the court system. In the meantime, she and Dana continued to squat.

EMILY BURNS LED THE way across the grounds of Glenburnie carrying a lamp. Pearls and "Poe" carried the bloodied corpse of Jennie Merrill and

Main Street, Natchez. *Lucius Marion Lampton, MD Historical Images Collection. Mississippi State University Libraries.*

dumped it in a thicket before taking off. Dick and Octavia simply walked next door to Glenwood.

Clearly, the fivesome was not experienced in the ways of murder. Jennie Merrill's body was found the next day. Dick and Octavia were immediately identified as suspects.

When the authorities arrived at Glenwood, it became only a matter of time before Natchez—and the rest of the country—was introduced to the real Dick Dana and Octavia Dockery.

When investigators and reporters walked into Glenwood, they walked into another world—a dark, Gothic juxtaposition that would have been at home in the fiction of Flannery O'Connor, Cormac McCarthy or William Faulkner.

The once beautiful Glenwood was falling apart—anyone walking by over the past decade could see that. What the investigators were not prepared for was the interior.

The inside was a garbage heap of decayed, decaying and rotted furniture. Fleas and rats and even snakes had free rein of the place. There were bird droppings and animal feces everywhere. But most astonishing were the goats. There were goats in the yard, in the living room, upstairs, on the balcony and in the bedrooms. They wandered around with a sense of entitlement, oblivious to investigators and reporters.

One reporter summed up the interior thusly: "It is a mansion of contrasts—marble and muck, rosewood furniture and debris, priceless canopied four-posted beds stand on crumbling floors. Dirt that accumulated when Natchez-Under-the-Hill was a famous river town is ankle deep in the great old halls where once gathered the gentry of the Mississippi to sip mint julips."[180] Another wrote: "'Goat Castle,' with its accumulation of debris which seems to have been untouched for 40 years, does more to tell the tragic futility of the lives of the man who might have been a world-famous musician and the woman who was once a leader in the social life of the aristocratic old Natchez of the past."[181]

The soon-to-be famous novelist, Gwen Bristow, came to Natchez as a reporter for the *Times-Picayune*. She, too, was astonished with the condition of Glenwood. "Edgar Allen Poe never described a place such as the 'Goat Castle,' because he never saw its equal.…Chickens and ducks run in and out of the doorway and flutter over the furniture in the hall with easy familiarity. Cats scramble over the sofa in front of the parlor." The couple cooked their meals in the marble fireplace beneath a bust of Charles Dickens and a large portrait of the Reverend Charles Dana. Pinecones and kindling covered the furniture. Bristow found a second cooking station upstairs when she stumbled upon a large piece of a recently slaughtered goat on some bedsprings. Evidently, Octavia used the springs to roast her and Dick's meals.

The condition of their house complemented the ugly crime that had been committed next door. Dick and Octavia were promptly arrested for the murder of their nemesis, Jennie Merrill. The evidence quickly established their guilt. But the guilty couple did have one advantage: they were White; their three accomplices were not.

From prison, Octavia Dockery immediately began to garner sympathy. She played the role of the falsely accused, distressed belle to a tee. For many, she became the personification of the Old South. Like many of that romantic time, Octavia Dockery was a victim of circumstance, a once beautiful and talented Scarlet O'Hara whose promise was snuffed out by an invading army seven decades before. She was a living Windsor Ruins.

One week after her arrest and subsequent imprisonment, she told a reporter:

> *I was born on the ancestral estate of my father, Thomas Blaine Dockery, who was a brigadier general in the Confederate army.…For a time I lived*

Main Street, Natchez. *Lucius Marion Lampton, MD Historical Images Collection. Mississippi State University Libraries.*

the life of a political butterfly. My brother-in-law occupied a position of considerable prominence in the community and I had no cares beyond the effort to amuse myself. Frequently I traveled to Vicksburg and New Orleans to attend balls and house parties of friends….I decided after my return to Natchez to establish a chicken farm on the property of Dick Dana who was then a prominent planter. What else was there to do? I must earn my daily bread.

They say that I killed Miss Merrill. That's not true. I intend to prove my innocence, although I have very little money some of my relatives and friends in the north, friends of the old days when I was a southern belle, will help me fight my case.[182]

Dick Dana followed Octavia's lead and likewise played the role of southern gentry fallen on hard times.

For a time I studied music in New York and sang in the choir of Christ church. Before my hand was injured by a falling window, I had considerable reputation as a pianist. In my young days my musical ability made me a social favorite. I was much sought after because I could entertain in the drawing rooms. I was fond of society, prided myself on my appearance, and considered myself a man of parts. I did not shun social contacts in those days, for it was impressed upon my mind that no true Southern gentleman would be a "stick."[183]

Public opinion quickly shifted in favor of the conspirators. Two weeks later, Judge Richard Cutrer released Octavia and Dick from prison on their own recognizance. The packed courtroom erupted in cheers as well-wishers gathered around the beleaguered couple to congratulate them and shake their hands. A few even offered the eccentrics a place to stay. Instead, Octavia and Dick promptly returned to Glenwood.

OCTAVIA DOCKERY AND DICK Dana, bona fide southerners with Confederate pedigree, were indicted by a grand jury, but the district attorney refused to prosecute the case.[184] At a second trial a year later, a Natchez judge declared a mistrial, citing the inability to assemble an Adams County jury. After three hundred potential jurors were examined, only five could be found who didn't

1927 flood refugee sewing tent. *Mississippi State University Libraries.*

already have an opinion on the case. When the judge made his decision, the courtroom erupted in applause, and many well-wishers escorted Octavia and Dick back to Goat Castle. They were never convicted of the murder they had instigated and helped arrange.[185]

George Pearls, the gunman, immediately fled to Arkansas, where he was shot to death by a police officer three days after shooting Jennie Merrill.[186]

Edward Allen Poe Newell was arrested and held in jail but never formally charged. Two months later, he was released after being "fully investigated." (Perhaps his job as an undertaker and consequent reputation as one of "the good, gainfully employed Negroes" saved him.)

Emily Burns, who testified that she was present and that George Pearls was the gunman, was the only one convicted of Jennie Merrill's murder. She served eight years at the notorious Parchman Prison until she was finally reprieved by Governor Paul Johnson in 1940. She returned home to Natchez, where she remarried and became a mother in the Antioch Baptist Church—a sure sign of the respect with which she was held in Natchez's Black community. Emily Burns died in 1969, just long enough to witness the beginning of the end of Jim Crow.[187]

The "Goat Castle Murder" and its subsequent trial caught the attention of the nation. It involved six persons, three Black, three White. All, excepting the murdered Jennie Merrill, were guilty in one way or another. And yet, it was the other two White persons involved who profited. Newell was imprisoned, interrogated and eventually released. Burns served eight years in prison, and Pearls was shot resisting arrest. While it's true that Dockery and Dana spent more than a year defending themselves in court, there is no doubt that the trial brought them a notoriety-turned-celebrity they would not otherwise have achieved. Certainly, the income that came from interviews, appearances, fundraising and tours greatly supplemented their nonexistent income.

How did two such impoverished, reclusive, unpopular murderers win the affection of their community? No doubt, the Lost Cause mythology played its part. Octavia Dockery (General Thomas Dockery's daughter) and Dick Dana (the son of Robert E. Lee's chaplain), came to exemplify the tragedy that had befallen the South.[188]

The South was just beginning to get back on its economic feet when it was hammered by the Great Depression. The murder of Jennie Merrill occurred in the midst of this national disaster. It was a time of trial for newspapers as well, which struggled to sell copies to people who needed to save every possible penny for necessities. In order to survive, many papers began reporting salacious and entertaining tales of murder and outlaws. It was the era of John Dillinger, Pretty Boy Floyd and Bonnie and Clyde. The "Goat Castle Murder" was exactly what the nation craved.

Just as many poor and downtrodden began to sympathize and even root for the outlaw, so, too, did they begin to pity the down-on-their-luck eccentric couple at Goat Castle. Dockery and Dana had the added advantage of their Confederate pedigree, which endeared them to many of their fellow southerners.

And then there was human nature. Mankind is naturally drawn to beauty. It is also drawn to the grotesque. Our souls are drawn to the beautiful, but we also have a "fascination with the abomination." We read *Chicken Noodle Soup for the Soul* and Edgar Allen Poe. We laud *It's a Wonderful Life* and *Scarface*. We watch Oprah and the twin train wrecks of reality television and national news.

Natchez possesses its own beauty and abomination. People from all over the country flocked to see some of the nation's most beautiful homes. They also flocked to see the spectacle that was Goat Castle.

CHAPTER 10

THE TRAGEDY

A Fire Wounds Natchez, and the Nation

The night were calm and beautiful,
The skies were bright and fair,
The crowd were being jubilant
And knew not death were there.

They were eating and drinking and smoking,
Dancing and having a time,
And in less than half an hour, brethren,
Hundreds of people were dying.
—*Charles Haffer Jr., "The Natchez Fire Disaster," 1942*[189]

The Moneywasters Social Club wanted to bring big acts to Natchez. Other cities in Mississippi—Jackson, McComb, Vicksburg, Yazoo City—had joined the Chitlin' Circuit in the past few years, drawing jazz acts from around the country. The Moneywasters wanted to bring those acts—no, bigger acts—to their ramshackle metal-clad building on St. Catherine Street. The building had been a church, a hardware store and even a blacksmith's shop. Now, it was a place for the Moneywasters to drink and gamble.

The Moneywasters Social Club was made up of thirteen "good-time Charleys," as one magazine described them. The goal of their club was to have fun and to share a little fun with the nearly ten thousand Black citizens of Natchez. In 1938, they decided they'd like to try making a little money.

A promotional photo of Walter Barnes. *Flickr user Bunky's Pickle.*

They hung a Jax beer sign above the front door of the building, christened it the "Rhythm Club" and began inviting the public to attend dances there.

Jazz acts from Chicago and other parts of the Midwest and the South had figured out in the previous decade that they could do well playing "one night stands" in small, Black towns around the South. No town seemed too small to host a jazz act, and no venue seemed too rustic. Within a year, the Rhythm Club had started to book "stars" like Andy Kirk and Floyd Smith of the Twelve Clouds of Joy.[190]

The Moneywasters thought they were ready for one of the biggest stars of all. For years, they had seen ads in the *Chicago Defender*—one of the prominent Black newspapers of the time—calling for "any and all dance promoters" to get in touch. The call had been made week after week by one of the *Defender*'s writers, who also happened to be one of the biggest jazz stars in the country: Walter Barnes. The Moneywasters wanted Barnes.[191]

Walter Barnes was a Mississippi boy, having grown up in Vicksburg. But Chicago called. Barnes, still in high school when he moved there in 1922, thought he would be an auto mechanic. But his love of music pulled him toward the life of a performer. He took classes at the Chicago Musical College and the Coleridge-Taylor School of Music. His talent at playing saxophone was apparent, and he soon found himself a member of Jelly Roll Morton's band.

He spent the next few years playing in Chicago's clubs, eventually becoming the leader of his own band. Barnes's music was upbeat and rhythmic, with tuba and cornet providing plenty of respective low and high notes. Lyrics were catchy but sparse; in "Buffalo Rhythm," the whirling music is only interrupted twice for a chorus of "hot deedle hot deedle hot deedle hot deedle hot deedle dot dee deedle dot dee ow." It was celebratory music that had the verve of champagne bubbling in a flute.[192]

Early in Barnes's career, he had found a patron in Al Capone and support from the Music Corporation of America. He made his name playing at Capone's Cotton Club in Cicero, Illinois. But within a few years, his support from Capone and the MCA dried up.

Barnes realized he could earn more on the road and exert more influence as a writer for the *Defender*. He began extensively touring the South and Midwest and wintering in Jacksonville, Florida, where he developed an enthusiastic fan base. His musical success brought him wealth. He began carrying hundreds of dollars in cash in his pocket. While other jazz acts toured in crowded buses, Barnes traveled in a gold Nash with swooping fenders, sleeping in the back seat while his wife drove.

He had conquered the Chicago music scene and now the Chitlin' Circuit. In fact, he had practically created the Chitlin' Circuit.

The little maestro with a friendly smile (complete with a gold front tooth) agreed to add Natchez to the end of his 1939–40 tour. He would extend his tour just a bit and play the Rhythm Club on April 23, 1940, with his orchestra of around a dozen musicians. He had planned on being back in Chicago by April 24, but the Natchez gig would delay him only a few days. The gig in Natchez would allow him to stop by his hometown of Vicksburg the next day.

Barnes coming to Natchez was a big deal, and not only because he was such a famous jazz leader. His work for the *Defender* made him one of the most influential jazz writers of the era. He would tour and write about the places he visited. In every town, he would name one street "the stroll"—the place where Black citizens could gather for a good time. Farish

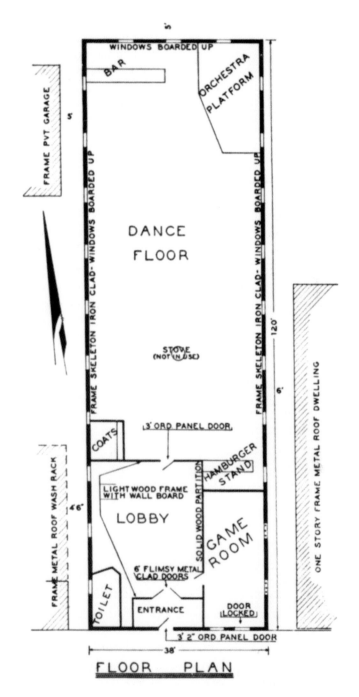

A floor plan of the Rhythm Club originally published in a 1940 National Fire Protection Association booklet. *Internet Archive.*

Street was the stroll in Jackson, Mississippi; Rampart Street was the stroll in New Orleans. Pascagoula, Mississippi, had beautiful creole women. There was a great restaurant in Monroe, Louisiana, called the Grog Cafe. Barnes's columns in the *Defender* constituted a guide for Black musicians looking to tour the South.

His visit to Natchez, then, would be a major entertainment milestone but would also put Natchez on the map for readers of the *Defender*. Bringing Barnes to Natchez was a coup for the Moneywasters, the Rhythm Club and the city.[193]

THE RHYTHM CLUB MIGHT have been a little rough looking from the outside, with its corrugated iron sheathing and barnlike shape. The building was a 124-by-36-foot rectangle. But inside, it actually had some of the amenities of a real dance hall. The Moneywasters had installed a hardwood dance floor. Some thought had been given to decorating. A bar, stocked with soft drinks and sandwiches, offered refreshments to dancers.

A photo of the Rhythm Club taken after the fire, originally published in a 1940 National Fire Protection Association booklet. *Internet Archive.*

Ed Frazier, vice president of the Moneywasters and manager of the club, wanted to take extra care to make the place inviting. The Moneywasters strung chicken wire between the rafters of the building, then wove flowers and Spanish moss through the wire and down the walls. The moss and wire barrier effectively lowered the high ceiling of the club to eight feet, lower than the average ceiling height of a residential home today. The mossy canopy would add a coziness and whimsy to the club.

Because Spanish moss was believed to harbor chiggers, the decorations were treated with a petroleum-based insecticide called Flit. The Moneywasters placed an exhaust fan at the rear of the club to keep the air in the building circulating. They would charge fifty cents a head for admission to Barnes's show and expected several hundred to attend. That would net everyone involved in putting on the show a lot of money, and they wanted to ensure they received every penny they were due. Although the Rhythm Club had a back entrance, it was bolted prior to the show. Any windows to the outside were barred. No one would be getting in—or even peeping in—unless they paid their fifty cents and walked through the front door.[194]

It was April 23, the day of the big show. Woodrich McGuire, the handsome young violinist and bandmaster at Brumfield High School, addressed his pupils. They should go and hear Walter Barnes play, McGuire told them. Barnes is a big deal, and him coming here is a big deal for Natchez. They should listen to Barnes carefully. Study his musical style and choreography.

Of course, McGuire was not telling his students anything they did not already know. The Moneywasters had spread word of the show far and wide. They had sold hundreds of advance tickets before the day of the show had even arrived.

High school students flocked to the Rhythm Club that night. The turnout must have surprised and delighted the Moneywasters. More than seven hundred people showed up. The sun set on Natchez, and people filled the Rhythm Club. Despite the fan blowing full speed, the club filled with tobacco smoke. Alcohol began to flow. Walter Barnes and the Royal Creolians set up. In all, the orchestra would have twelve members: Barnes as leader, a vocalist, four saxophonists, a guitarist, a trumpeter, a trombonist, a pianist, a bassist and a drummer.[195]

THE JITTERBUG WAS THE dance du jour in 1940. It was a couples' dance that necessitated quick footwork and incorporated moves called "peckin'," "boogie woogie," "swing the wing" and "whip the hip." As Walter Barnes and his large band began to play, the young members of the audience began to jitterbug—well, they tried to jitterbug as best they could. The truth was, so many people had packed into the Rhythm Club that dancing was not really possible.

It was spring in Natchez, but the night was hot. Though there was no room for dancing, the crowd enjoyed listening to Barnes, drinking beer, smoking and "laughing and grinning," as one attendee put it. The whirring fan did its best to move air through the room. The sounds of Barnes and his orchestra carried far beyond the metal walls of the Rhythm Club.

Eliza M. Wright was one of the young women inside the Rhythm Club that night. She had spent hours in the club with her husband, drinking and having a good time. As the night passed, Wright began to feel hungry. Across the street from the club, a restaurant was selling fried catfish. Wright and her husband left the club and ate their fill. Wright was ready to go back and have fun for a few more hours. She did make it back into the club. But something moved her husband to find her inside and get her out.

"My husband made me go home," she told an interviewer many years later. "He said, 'uh uh—you ain't gonna stay out here all night.' And he took me home."

Her husband's insistence that she leave the club likely saved her life.[196]

Natchez in 1935, by Ben Hahn. *Library of Congress.*

At around 11:30 p.m., Walter Barnes instructed his band to play "Clarinet Lullaby." His orchestra began playing the tune, but soon his drummer—so important for keeping rhythm in the band—faltered. Barnes, with his back to the crowd, was incensed. He glared at the drummer but realized that the members of his band were watching, wide-eyed, something terrible unfolding near the front of the building.

A survivor would later recount a feverish memory from the first moments of the catastrophe that would rapidly unfold inside the club. "You've set the place on fire," the witness thought he remembered a young woman remarking to her friend as the pair exited the bathroom. A string of Spanish moss hanging down one of the walls caught fire, probably from a careless cigarette, and like a fuse burning to its charge climbed its way up to the moss canopy of the building.

People near the front door, where the fire started, began to shout and cry. Someone yelled "Fire!," and the people lucky enough to be standing near the front door left the building without trouble. James "Boots" Jordan was one of them. He sent word to summon the fire department then began trying to fight the fire himself. When the fire began to get worse, Jordan helped some people outside.

People farther back in the club at first thought the commotion came from one of the fights that inevitably broke out during big dances. Within moments, though, there was no doubt what was happening.

The ventilation fan fed oxygen to the fire. "There was a hissing roar like a heavy gust of wind blowing through a forest," a witness recounted to a reporter days later, "and the entire inside of the building appeared to be filled with flame and smoke."

The sudden conflagration sent people rushing toward the front entrance—the only way out.

Barnes, still half-directing his orchestra, tried to urge the crowd to stay calm. "You can all get out if you keep calm," he shouted. Barnes had seen fires in places like this before and knew they could usually be put out if calm heads acted quickly. But he had never seen a fire like this. Most of his orchestra tried to continue playing, but his drummer, who happened to have a hammer, abandoned the group and headed for a back window.

Three Alcorn College students, arm in arm, were the last able to leave the front doorway before it became tangled with panicked, injured and dying people. The realization that the front door was now impassable triggered a stampede to the back of the building. As people ran, a "seething, blistering

Natchez in 1935, by Ben Hahn. *Library of Congress.*

curtain of death" fell. Some people found themselves pinned to the floor by the stampede and trampled to death.

In the rear of the building, they found a melee, as panicked people fought and rammed each other trying to escape. As the metal walls of the building radiated intense heat, people tore their clothes off trying to cool down. The back section of the building turned into a deathtrap.

Some lucky ones were able to escape through windows that had been battered open by strong, brave people with the presence of mind to act fast.

Johnny Jones, a bartender at the club, was one such person. Using his knee as a battering ram, he managed to smash one of the windows open. Choking on smoke and bleeding from an injury, he helped four young women out the window before climbing through himself and falling, unconscious, to the ground.

Walter Audrey, another bartender, made it through a window and helped to disentangle and help six others who were trying to push through the window. George Minor, a high school student, used a chair to break open another window, saving himself and his sister. Willie Simmons was able to push his wife through a window but did not have the strength to escape himself.

Astonishingly, Boots Jordan, the man who had tried to fight the fire in its earliest stage, had run back into the building to try to break open some of the back windows. His last moments were spent trying to save others.

Oscar Brown, the drummer for Barnes's orchestra, used his hammer to bash open another window and escape—he would be one of only two members of the band to make it out alive. The other was Walter Barnes's brother Alan, who happened to be on the band's bus when the fire started. Walter Barnes and the rest of the band members would die on the bandstand, choked and suffocated by smoke.[197]

Jessie Craig, a Natchez teacher, had the presence of mind to shove her head into the club's icebox. She waited out the fire, losing consciousness and receiving severe burns but keeping her life. Woodrich McGuire, the high school band teacher who had urged his pupils to attend the show that night, was not so lucky.

Firefighters—with a station only four blocks away—arrived quickly, tapped into a water main and began spraying the fire. Though they did not realize it at the moment, the water spraying on the hot sheet metal created steam, adding a deadly new element to the disaster. As firefighters beat the flames back, they tried to enter the building but realized that piled bodies would not allow them to easily penetrate the building. Nevertheless, they would extinguish the fire within a half an hour.

Ed Frazier, the Moneywaster and manager of the Rhythm Club, had made it out of the building. His wife did not. As he stood on the sidewalk with the fire raging, his heart simply stopped working, and he fell to the ground, dead.[198]

It would take days for the true toll of the fire to be known. In all, the fire claimed 209 lives, making it the fourth-deadliest fire in American history to the present day.[199]

IN THE AFTERMATH OF the fire, people asked the obvious question: How could this have happened? It was clear that the Moneywasters had made a grave and stupid mistake by blocking egress to the building. In the aftermath of the fire, the mayor of Natchez described the Rhythm Club as "the worst fire trap imaginable." But why had someone—some official body—not recognized that fact prior to the tragedy? Why had it been allowed to happen? The Natchez coroner announced a few days after the fire that the disaster had been an accident. But he did not speak to the negligence of those responsible for the Rhythm Club's setup.[200]

Walter Barnes was buried in Chicago a week after the Rhythm Club fire. Thirty thousand people viewed his body as it rested at the W.T. Brown Jr. Mortuary. Alan, the brother who had narrowly avoided Walter's fate, was there beside him. Walter Barnes was only thirty-three when he died but had accomplished more in his short life than most could ever dream.[201]

A view from Natchez Under-the-Hill in 1972. *Library of Congress.*

The tragedy devastated the Black community of Natchez. The majority of the victims of the fire were under twenty-five, and many of them were local high school students. A hundred children lost their parents in the fire. Important members of the community—teachers, professionals, musicians, leaders—were suddenly gone. Many of those who survived bore the psychological and physical scars of the ordeal. The experience left a psychic wound on the entire community and seemed to annihilate the vibrant culture that had been developing on St. Catherine Street. When a pair of field recorders visited Natchez later that year to record local musicians, they found a town where no one was interested in playing "worl'ly" music. What was supposed to elevate Natchez's status in the music world had instead done the opposite.[202]

> *Night time is falling, day is almost done,*
> *My baby left last night; she left to have some fun.*
>
> *At two o'clock in the morning by the clock on the wall*
> *Yes, I thought I heard my poor baby call.*
>
> *Ooh, the nights are long; I can't sleep at all,*
> *Since my sweet mama burned in that Rhythm Hall.*
>
> *Yes, the day is breaking, sun refuse to shine,*
> *I'm leaving Natchez, Mississippi, moving on down the line.*
> *—Lewis Bronzeville Five, "Natchez Mississippi Blues," 1940*

NOTES

Chapter 1

1. The above echo the sentiments of the Natchez. It was the greed of Sieur de Chepart that drove the Natchez to eliminate what they saw as a French threat to their sovereignty.
2. Myers, *1729*, 83–4.
3. Ibid., 170.
4. Reeves, *Governors of Louisiana*, 13.
5. Myers, *1729*, 135.
6. French, *Historical Memoirs*, 77, quoted in Myers, 177.
7. Ibid., 177–178.
8. Dumont, *Memoir of Lieutenant Dumont*, 236, quoted in Myers, *1729*, 175 and 178.
9. Father le Petit, quoted in Myers, *1729*, 305.
10. Myers, *1729*, 174 (Milne 176).
11. Father Philiberts, "Victims of the 1729 Massacre at Natchez." From Ministry of the Colonies, National Archives of France, C. 13, V. 12, General Correspondence of Louisiana, pages 57–58 v.; copy Vol. XIX, pages 241–45, quoted in Myers, *1729*, 285.
12. Le Petit, 166, quoted in Myers, *1729*, 171–72.
13. Swanton, 239, quoted in Myers, *1729*, 197.
14. An unfortunate few of these captives would remain prisoners of the Choctaw for several more months until the French fulfilled their obligations to the former for all their service in recovering the captives in the first place (Myers, *1729*, 199).

Chapter 2

15. Many previously unpublished details of John Blommart's life in Natchez come from a collection of handwritten "memorials" assembled by the National Archives of the United Kingdom and digitized by Ancestry.com. In the collection of documents, Blommart gives a detailed account of his life from 1778 to 1781, much of which he spent in Natchez. Blommart originally testified to his experiences for the purpose of recouping a small fortune he had lost in service of the king during the Revolutionary War period, but the documents now give a detailed look at other facets of Blommart's life. American Loyalist Claims, 1776–1835, AO 12–13. The National Archives of the United Kingdom.

16. Arnold, "Quapaws and the American Revolution"; "Letter from Col. John Stuart to Henry Stuart."

17. Ibid.

18. Ibid.

19. Cleveland, "Only Tavern Left on Trace, Restored"; Pietsch, "Ships' Boys and Youth Culture in Eighteenth-Century Britain"; Smith, "Swiss Connection"; "Memorial of John Blommart, Esq."

20. Clowes, *Royal Navy*, 116–24.

21. Barker, "Naval Uniform Dress of 1748."

22. Dalrymple, ed., *Merchant of Manchac*, 143.

23. Ibid., 83–84.

24. Haynes, *Natchez District*, 18–20; Dalrymple, ed., *Merchant of Manchac*, 20–21.

25. "Inventory of the Estate of John Blommart."

26. Rea, "Redcoats and Redskins."

27. Haynes, *Natchez District*, 18–20; Miller, "Welcome to Mount Locust."

28. Starr, *Tories, Dons, and Rebels*, 108–10; Grant, "Anthony Hutchins."

29. Wright Jr., *Florida in the American Revolution*, 52–54.

30. Mitchell, "America's Spanish Savior."

31. Grant, "Natchez Revolt of 1781."

32. "Memorial of John Blommart, Esq."; Grant, "Natchez Revolt of 1781."

33. Ibid.

34. Ibid.

35. "Memorial of John Blommart, Esq."

Chapter 3

36. Hildreth, "History of an Early Voyage," 134–35.

37. Holmes, *Gayoso*, 116–17.

38. Moore, *Natchez Under-the-Hill*, 35–6.

39. Ibid., 38–9.

40. Ibid.

41. Cist, *Cincinnati Miscellany*, 125–26.

42. "Flat Boats," *Tallow Light*.

43. Ibid.

44. Ingraham, *South-west*, 19–20.

45. Johnson, *William Johnson's Natchez*, 94, 171, 175, 177, 205, 212, 259.

46. Moore, *Natchez Under-the-Hill*, 38–9.

47. "Last of the Boatmen," *National Gazette*.

48. "Natchez, M.T.," *Washington Republican and Natchez Intelligencer*, May 28, 1817.

49. Dayton, *Steamboat Days*, 332–35.

50. Phelps, "Stands and Travel Accommodations."

51. Holden, "Along the Ole Natchez Trace"; Bradley, Harrison and Barker, Map of the United States.

52. Coates, *Outlaw Years*, 88–105.

53. Ludlow, "Account of the Mail Robbery."

54. Coates, *Outlaw Years*, 88–105.

55. Bertram, "At Home on the Trace."

56. Phelps, "Stands and Travel Accommodations."

57. Dayton, *Steamboat Days*, 332–35.

Chapter 4

58. Alford, *Prince among Slaves*, 32–6 and 41–4.

59. Ibid., 48–9.

60. Antebellum geologist B.L.C. Wailes claims that "[Indigo] killed every Negro employed in its culture in the short space of five years." (Alford, *Prince among Slaves*, 49.)

61. Alford, *Prince among Slaves*, 44.

62. Ibid., 21–2.

63. Ibid., 46.

64. Ibid., 47.

65. Ibid., 17–8.

66. Ibid., 68.

67. Ibid., 82–4 and 118–20.

68. Ibid., 101–02.

69. Ibid., 183.

Chapter 5

70. Daniels, *Devil's Backbone*, 95.
71. Caughey, *Bernardo De Galvez*, 102–03.
72. DuVal, *Independence Lost*, 122.
73. During the American Revolutionary War, Florida was divided into two colonies: East and West Florida. In 1775, both were British colonies.
74. Because Spain was officially at peace with Great Britain, Galvez offered sanctuary to British subjects fleeing the rebel Willing. Willing took property from the British side but also from British subjects residing in Spanish territory—a clear violation of Spanish sovereignty.
75. Haynes, *Natchez District*, 97–9.
76. The American general George Rogers Clarke summed up Willing's raid: "When plunder is the prevailing Passion of any Body of Troops wheather Great or Small, their Cuntrey can Expect but little service from them Which I am Sorry to find was too Much the Case with the party.... Floriday on the Mississippi Might have been good subjects to the States if proper Measures had been taken and probably saved the Expence of a Campaign."
77. In 1780 and 1781, with Spain and Britain finally at war, Galvez launched a campaign that captured both Natchez and Pensacola. Despite his penchant for humanity and fairness, the citizens of West Florida rallied behind King George. No doubt, the behavior of James Willing had something to do with the sudden surge of loyalty to His Britannic Majesty.
78. King, "Real Philip Nolan," 103.
79. Ibid., 92.
80. Jackson, "Nolan Expeditions."
81. King, "Real Philip Nolan," 94.
82. Ibid., 95.
83. Ibid.
84. King, "Real Philip Nolan," 100.
85. Ibid., 101.
86. Daniels, *Devil's Backbone*, 95–6.
87. King, "Real Philip Nolan," 104.
88. Jackson, "Nolan Expeditions."
89. Bean, *Memoir of Colonel Ellis P. Bean*, 3–4.
90. Ibid., 6–7. The survivors of Nolan's party surrendered, including the seventeen-year-old, second in command, former flatboat man Ellis Peter Bean. After years in captivity, Bean returned to the United States and published an account of his adventure. He does not paint President Thomas Jefferson in a sympathetic light: "I must inform my reader that we

had passed five years, in all, in Mexico; that our cases in this time had gone to Spain; and had also been sent to the United States, and laid before Mr. Jefferson, at that time president—who said he knew nothing of us, and that we should be tried according to the Spanish laws....As Mr. Jefferson did not know us, and had no expectation of being benefited by us, it was less trouble to say, 'Hang them!'" (Bean, *Memoir of Colonel Ellis P. Bean*, 12.)

91. Davis, *Three Roads*, 163–64, 207.
92. Ibid., 214.
93. Ibid., 214–17. The above vignette on James Bowie in Natchez is taken exclusively from William C. Davis's *Three Roads to the Alamo*. Obviously, relying on one source is not ideal—unless that source is Davis. In fact, we strongly believe William C. Davis is one of the most well-documented, readable writers of history. His account of the sandbar fight between Natchez and Vidalia is the authoritative account of this famous and disputed duel.
94. Davis, *Three Roads*, 248.
95. Ibid., 55–9.
96. The above sentence just might be the first time the words *permanent* and *Bowie* were used in the same sentence.
97. Davis, *Three Roads*, 245–46, 249.
98. May, *John A. Quitman*, 238.
99. Caldwell, "Lopez Expeditions To Cuba," 58; *American Citizen* (Canton, MS), June 8, 1850.
100. May, *John A. Quitman*, 197.
101. Ibid., 205; "Presidential Candidates," *Vicksburg Daily Whig*, December 18, 1855.
102. May, *John A. Quitman*, 238–39.
103. Lopez's standard was what eventually became the official flag of Cuba.
104. May, *John A. Quitman*, 252.
105. Caldwell, "Lopez Expeditions to Cuba," 84.
106. *Mississippi Free Trader* (Natchez), May 27, 1854; May, *John A. Quitman*, 277–78.
107. May, *John A. Quitman*, 278.
108. Ibid., 279–81.
109. Ibid., 293.
110. Ibid., 295.

Chapter 6

111. Davis, *Black Experience in Natchez*, 74.
112. Alford, *Prince among Slaves*, 29–30.

113. Slave Voyages.
114. *Mississippi Free Trader* (Natchez), December 25, 1850.
115. The present-day sight is at the intersection of Liberty Road and D'Evereux Drive/St. Catherine Street.
116. D'Evereux, Linden and Monmouth Plantations, all of which still stand today, were each within eyesight of the slave market in the 1830s.
117. Hannah Natanson, *Washington Post*, September 14, 2019. "They were once America's cruelest, richest slave traders. Why does no one know their names? Isaac Franklin and John Armfield committed atrocities they appeared to relish."
118. Wascom, *Blood of Heaven*, 167.
119. Davis, *Black Experience in Natchez*, 75–6.
120. Ibid., 76.
121. Ibid., 71–2.
122. Ibid., 67.
123. Ibid., 15.
124. Tanner, ed., *Chained to the Land*, 15–17. In the 1930s, the WPA sent a number of interviewers to Louisiana and Mississippi to gather oral histories of the formerly enslaved. Although these interviews recall events from seventy years before, and in many cases were from a child's or a grandchild's recalling of their parents' and grandparents' reminiscences, they are still a very valuable piece to understanding antebellum days.
125. Michener, *Drifters*, 119. "The three most important building blocks of American history are black: anthracite, petroleum, slaves."
126. Davis, *Black Experience in Natchez*, 91–2.
127. Walker, *Jubilee*, 486.

Chapter 7

128. Johnson, *William Johnson's Natchez*, 52.
129. Ibid., 223–24.
130. Ibid., 182–83.
131. Davis and Hogan, *Barber of Natchez*, 200–1.
132. Johnson, *William Johnson's Natchez*, 265–67.
133. Ibid., 267.
134. *Transactions of the American Medical Association*, 524.
135. History of Mississippi, "Yellow Fever Epidemic," http://sites.rootsweb.com/~msalhn/yellowfever.html.
136. Johnson, *William Johnson's Natchez*, 265–66.
137. Ibid., 267–68.

138. Ibid., 268, footnote 15.

139. Ibid., 280.

140. "Dreadful Visitation of Providence," *Weekly Mississippian*, May 15, 1840 (from *Natchez Free Trader Extra*, May 8, 1840).

141. Ibid.

142. Ibid.

143. Ibid.

144. Johnson, *William Johnson's Natchez*, 280.

145. Ibid., 280–81.

146. Ibid., 280, footnote 6.

147. Davis and Hogan, *Barber of Natchez*, 76.

148. Davis, *Black Experience in Natchez*, 59.

149. *Natchez Daily Courier*, June 20, 1851.

150. Davis and Hogan, *Barber of Natchez*, 267–71.

151. Davis, *Black Experience in Natchez*, 65.

152. Davis and Hogan, *Barber of Natchez*, 227.

Chapter 8

153. Moore, ed., *Rebellion Record*, 377–78.

154. Ibid.; Barr, *Polignac's Texas Brigade*, 36–7; Moore, ed., *Rebellion Record*, 377–78.

155. "Suicide of Col. McCaleb," *Henry Republic*.

156. "Skirmish at Vidalia: Report of Lt. Col. Hubert A. McCaleb, Second Mississippi Heavy Artillery, African Descent." *The War of the Rebellion: A Compilation of the Official Records of the Union and Confederate Armies, Series I, Vol. XXXIV, Part I* (Washington, D.C.: Government Printing Office, 1891). 129–130.

157. Barr, *Polignac's Texas Brigade*, 36–37; Moore, ed., *Rebellion Record*, 377–78.

158. *War of the Rebellion*, "Skirmish at Vidalia: Report of Lt. Col. Hubert A. McCaleb, Second Mississippi Heavy Artillery, African Descent," 129–30.

159. *Union Army*, 900–1.

160. Davis, *Black Experience in Natchez*, 165.

161. Behrend, "Rebellious Talk and Conspiratorial Plots."

162. Ibid.

163. Ibid.

164. Davis, *Black Experience in Natchez*, 165–79.

165. "Bernard G. Farrar, Jr. Collection," University of Missouri–Kansas City.

166. "Colonel Farrar and Some Negro Troops Make a Descent Upon a Rebel Dancing Party," *Philadelphia Inquirer*, January 2, 1864.

167. Davis, *Black Experience in Natchez*, 165–79.

168. "Colonel Farrar and Some Negro Troops," *Philadelphia Inquirer*.

Chapter 9

169. "Dana Scores in Jackson Recital: Natchez 'Wild Man' and Miss Dockery Given Warm Reception Here," *Clarion-Ledger*, October 28, 1932.

170. "Dana Drops 'Wild Man' Role, Plans to Tour South," *Times Picayune*, September 18, 1932.

171. Cox, *Goat Castle*, 36–46.

172. Ibid., 47–50.

173. Ibid., 30–1, 38.

174. Kane, *Natchez on the Mississippi*, location 5158.

175. Ibid., location 5164.

176. Ibid., location 5277.

177. Cox, *Goat Castle*, 65.

178. "Officials Still Say Case Open," *Clarion-Ledger*, August 25, 1932.

179. "Find New Clues to Mystery: Peculiar Finger-Prints May Identify Merrill Murderer," *Clarion-Ledger*, August 8, 1932.

180. "Dana, Miss Dockery Return to Squalor and Musty Grandeur of Their Goat Castle: Strange Natchez Couple Back in Mansion of Marble and Muck, Rosewood Furniture and Debris," *Town Talk* (Alexandria, VA), August 17, 1932.

181. "Life Story of Richard Dana Document of Tragic Futility," *Shreveport Journal*, August 9, 1932.

182. "Finger Prints Hold Eccentric in Murder Case: Natchez Officers Announce That Miss Octavia Dockery and R.H. Dana Will Be Charged in Crime," *Greenwood Commonwealth*, August 10, 1932.

183. "Life Story of Richard Dana," *Shreveport Journal*.

184. Ferranti, "These White People Profited off Their Neighbor's Murder."

185. "'Goat Castle' Case Ends in a Mistrial: Failure to Get Jury in Dockery Case, Judge Rules a Mistrial," *Winona (MS) Times*, December 1, 1933.

186. "Finger Prints Key to Mystery: But Just Who Made Prints at Merrill Home Is Another Matter," *Courier News* (Blytheville, AR), August 20, 1932. Lawrence Williams, a known Chicago criminal who used the aliases "Pinkey Williams" and "George Pearls," was killed while in possession of the same type of gun used to kill Jennie Merrill.

187. While the *Greenwood Commonwealth* (August 23, 1932) records her confession, there are some who believed Emily Burns was coerced into a confession, as her fingerprints were never found in the house nor on the

lamp she claimed she had carried for Pearls and Poe. Governor Johnson was convinced of her innocence. He explained his decision to release her: "When I am convinced that I am right, no man or a group of men can put pressure on me to make me change my mind" (Cox, *Goat Castle*, 166).

188. Karen L. Cox claims, "They were not exactly local heroes, but the community felt sympathy toward them because they had come from respected families and were now living like paupers in complete filth. It was their lineage and race that ultimately spared them" (Ferranti, "These White People Profited off Their Neighbor's Murder").

Chapter 10

189. Springer, ed., *Nobody Knows Where the Blues Come From*, 86–87.

190. "Guitar Player Has Made Band 'Big Time'," *Pittsburgh Courier*, July 8, 1939.

191. Lauterbach, *Chitlin' Circuit and the Road to Rock 'n' Roll*, 31–72; "Rhythm in Natchez," *Time*, May 6, 1940.

192. Walter Barnes and His Royal Creolians, "Buffalo Rhythm," 1929, Internet Archive, https://archive.org.

193. Lauterbach, *Chitlin' Circuit and the Road to Rock 'n' Roll*, 31–72; "Chi Bows Head as Walter Comes Home—a Hero!," *Pittsburgh Courier*, May 4, 1940.

194. McCoy, "Natchez Night Club Was 'Worst Fire Trap'"; Burch, *Rhythm Club Fire*; Lauterbach, *Chitlin' Circuit and the Road to Rock 'n' Roll*, 31–72; "Rhythm in Natchez," *Time*, May 6, 1940.

195. "The Dead in Natchez Disaster," *Pittsburgh Courier*, May 4, 1940.

196. Burch, *Rhythm Club Fire*; "Teacher Tells of Fight at Rhythm Club Window," *Pittsburgh Courier*, May 11, 1940.

197. Williams, "Natchez Quivers in Stunned Grief"; McCoy, "Natchez Night Club Was 'Worst Fire Trap'"; Lauterbach, *Chitlin' Circuit and the Road to Rock 'n' Roll*, 66–69; "Survivors Tell of Fight at Natchez Fire," *Delta Democrat-Times* (Greenville, MS), April 25, 1940; "Put Her Head in Dance Hall Ice-Box; Lived," *Pittsburgh Courier*, May 11, 1940; Dumas Sr., "Local Boy Blows Last Note As 198 Die in Natchez Fire."

198. Burch, *Rhythm Club Fire*.

199. "Deadliest Public Assembly and Nightclub Fires," National Fire Protection Association.

200. "Fire Trap," *South Bend (IN) Tribune*, April 26, 1940; O.C.W. Taylor, "Disaster Suspects Released," *Pittsburgh Courier*, May 4, 1940.

201. "15,000 Attend Rites for Walter Barnes," *Negro Star*, May 10, 1940.

202. Joos, "Natchez Fire"; "100 Children Made Orphans," *Pittsburgh Courier*, May 11, 1940.

Bibliography

Articles

Arnold, Morris S., "The Quapaws and the American Revolution." *Arkansas Historical Quarterly* 79, no. 1 (March 1, 2020).

Barker, Derek. "The Naval Uniform Dress of 1748." *Mariner's Mirror* 65, no. 3 (1979).

Behrend, Justin. "Rebellious Talk and Conspiratorial Plots: The Making of a Slave Insurrection in Civil War Natchez." *Journal of Southern History* 77, no. 1 (2011).

Bertram, Jack. "At Home on the Trace." *Clarion-Ledger*, June 6, 2000.

Carter, Lucie Monk. "Murder, She Wrote: Another Look Inside Goat Castle Finds Justice for Its Victims." *Country Roads*, September 21, 2018.

Cleveland, Jim. "Only Tavern Left on Trace, Restored." *Clarion-Ledger*, May 20, 1962.

Davis, Ronald L.F. *The Black Experience in Natchez*. Natchez, MS: United States Department of the Interior, 1993.

Delta Democrat-Times. "Survivors Tell of Fight at Natchez Fire." April 25, 1940.

Dumas, A.W., Sr. "Local Boy Blows Last Note As 198 Die in Natchez Fire." *Indianapolis Recorder*, April 27, 1940.

"Flat Boats." *Tallow Light* 43, no. 3 (2012).

Grant, Ethan A. "Anthony Hutchins: A Pioneer of the Old Southwest." *Florida Historical Quarterly* 74, no. 4 (1996).

———. "The Natchez Revolt of 1781: A Reconsideration." *Mississippi Journal of History* 57, no. 4 (1994).

Hildreth, S.P. "History of an Early Voyage on the Ohio and Mississippi Rivers." *American Pioneer* 1 (1842).

Holden, Robert J. "Along the Ole Natchez Trace." *Simpson County News*, October 5, 1978 and November 9, 1978.

Joos, Vincent. "The Natchez Fire: African American Remembrance through Interviews, Photographs, and Songs." *Southern Quarterly* 50, no. 2 (2013).

Ludlow, Thomas W. "Account of the Mail Robbery." *Long Island Star*, March 18, 1818.

McCoy, J.R. "Natchez Night Club Was 'Worst Fire Trap.'" *Pittsburgh Courier*, May 4, 1940.

Miller, Robin. "Welcome to Mount Locust." *Town Talk*, July 18, 1999.

Mitchell, Barbara A. "America's Spanish Savior: Bernardo de Galvez." *Quarterly Journal of Military History* 23, no. 1 (2010).

National Gazette. "The Last of the Boatmen." December 30, 1828.

Phelps, Dawson A. "Stands and Travel Accommodations along the Natchez Trace." *Journal of Mississippi History* 10, no. 1 (1948).

Pietsch, Roland. "Ships' Boys and Youth Culture in Eighteenth-Century Britain: The Navy Recruits of the London Marine Society." *Northern Mariner* 14, no. 4 (2004).

Pittsburgh Courier. "Chi Bows Head as Walter Comes Home—A Hero!" May 4, 1940.

———. "The Dead in Natchez Disaster." May 4, 1940.

———. "Guitar Player Has Made Band 'Big Time.'" July 8, 1939.

———. "100 Children Made Orphans." May 11, 1940.

———. "Put Her Head in Dance Hall Ice-Box; Lived." May 11, 1940.

———. "Teacher Tells of Fight at Rhythm Club Window." May 11, 1940.

Rea, Robert R. "Redcoats and Redskins on the Lower Mississippi, 1763–1776." *Louisiana History* 11, no. 1 (1970).

Smith, Roger. "The Swiss Connection: International Networks in Some Eighteenth-Century Luxury Trades." *Journal of Design History* 17, no. 2 (2004).

Time. "Rhythm in Natchez." May 6, 1940.

Williams, John R. "Natchez Quivers in Stunned Grief as Dead Are Buried." *Pittsburgh Courier*, May 4, 1940.

Books

Alford, Terry. *Prince among Slaves: The True Story of an African Prince Sold into Slavery in the American South*. New York: Oxford University Press, 2007.

Barnett, James F., Jr. *The Natchez Indians: A History to 1735*. Jackson: University Press of Mississippi, 2007.

Barr, Alwyn. *Polignac's Texas Brigade*. College Station: Texas A&M University Press, 1998.

Bean, Ellis Peter. *Memoir of Colonel Ellis P. Bean, Written by Himself, About the Year 1816*. Republished from: *History of Texas from Its First Settlement in 1685 to Its Annexation to the United States in 1846*. Volume 1, Appendix No. II. N.p.: Henderson K. Yoakum, 1856.

Caldwell, Robert Grandville. "The Lopez Expeditions to Cuba 1848–1851." Dissertation, Princeton University, 1915.

Caughey, John Walton. *Bernardo De Galvez In Louisiana 1776–1783*. Gretna, LA: Pelican Publishing Company, 1998.

Cist, Charles. *Cincinnati Miscellany, or Antiquities of the West, and Pioneer History and General and Local Statistics*. Vol. 1. Cincinnati: C. Clark, 1846.

Clowes, Sir William Laird. *The Royal Navy: A History from the Earliest Times to the Present*. Vol. 3. London: Sampson Low, Marston and Company, 1898.

Coates, Robert M. *The Outlaw Years*. New York: Literary Guild of America, 1930.

Cox, Karen L. *Goat Castle: A True Story of Murder, Race, and the Gothic South*. Chapel Hill: University of North Carolina Press, 2017.

Dalrymple, Margaret Fisher, ed. *The Merchant of Manchac: The Letterbooks of John Fitzpatrick, 1768–1790*. Baton Rouge: Louisiana State University Press, 1978.

Daniels, Jonathan. *The Devil's Backbone: The Story of the Natchez Trace*. Gretna, LA: Pelican Publishing Company, 1998.

Davis, Edwin Adams, and William Ransom Hogan. *The Barber of Natchez*. Baton Rouge: Louisiana State University Press, 1997.

Davis, Ronald L.F. *The Black Experience in Natchez: 1720–1880*. Natchez, MS: Natchez Historical Park, 1993.

Davis, William C. *The Pirates Laffite: The Treacherous World of the Corsairs of the Gulf*. Orlando, FL: Harcourt Books, 2005.

———. *Three Roads to the Alamo: The Lives and Fortunes of David Crockett, James Bowie, and William Barret Travis*. New York: Harper Collins, 1998.

Dayton, Fred Erving. *Steamboat Days*. New York: Frederick A. Stokes Company, 1970.

Dumont, Jean-Francois-Benjamin. *The Memoir of Lieutenant Dumont, 1715–1747: A Sojourner in the French Atlantic*. Chapel Hill: University of North Carolina Press, 2012.

DuVal, Kathleen. *Independence Lost: Lives on the Edge of the American Revolution*. New York: Random House, 2015.

French, Benjamin Franklin. *Historical Memoirs of Louisiana, from the First Settlement of the Colony to the Departure of Governor O'Reilly in 1770*. Charleston, SC: Nabu Press, 2011.

Haynes, Robert V. *The Natchez District and the American Revolution*. Jackson: University of Mississippi, 1976.

Holmes, Jack D.L. *Gayoso: The Life of a Spanish Governor in the Mississippi Valley, 1789–1799.* Baton Rouge: Louisiana State University Press, 1965.

Ingraham, J.H. *The South-west.* New York: Harper Brothers, 1835.

Johnson, William, William Ransom Hogan and Edwin Adams Davis, eds. *William Johnson's Natchez: The Ante-Bellum Diary of a Free Negro.* Baton Rouge: Louisiana State University Press, 1993.

Kane, Harnett T. *Natchez on the Mississippi.* Aukland, NZ: Pickle Partners Publishing, 2016.

King, Grace. "The Real Philip Nolan." *Publications of the Louisiana Historical Society. New Orleans, Louisiana. Proceedings and Reports 1916.* Vol. 9. Louisiana Historical Society, 1917.

Lauterbach, Preston. *The Chitlin' Circuit and the Road to Rock 'n' Roll.* New York: W.W. Norton & Company, 2011.

May, Robert E. *John A. Quitman: Old South Crusader.* Baton Rouge: Louisiana State University, 1985.

Michener. James A. *The Drifters.* New York: Dial Press, 1971.

Moore, Edith Wyatt. *Natchez Under-the-Hill.* Natchez, MS: Southern Historical Publications, 1958.

Moore, Frank, ed. *The Rebellion Record: A Diary of American Events.* Vol. 8. New York: D. Van Nostrand, 1865.

Myers, Kenneth M. *1729: The True Story of Pierre & Marie Mayeux, the Natchez Massacre and the Settlement of French Louisiana.* Denison, TX: Mayeux Press, 2017.

Penicaut, André. *Fleur de Lys and Calumet: Being the Penicaut Narrative of French Adventure in Louisiana.* Translated and edited by Richebourg Gaillard McWilliams. Tuscaloosa: University of Alabama Press, 1981.

Reeves, Miriam G. *The Governors of Louisiana.* Gretna, LA: Pelican Publishing Company, 2004.

Springer, Robert, ed. *Nobody Knows Where the Blues Come From.* Jackson: University Press of Mississippi, 2006, 86–87.

Starr, J. Barton. *Tories, Dons, and Rebels: The American Revolution in British West Florida.* Gainesville: University Presses of Florida, 1976.

Tanner, Lynette Ater, ed. *Chained to the Land: Voices from Cotton & Cane Plantations.* Winston-Salem, NC: John F. Blair, 2014.

The Transactions of the American Medical Association. Instituted 1847. Vol. 7. New York: Baker, Godwin & Company, 1854.

The Union Army: A History of Military Affairs in the Loyal States, 1861–1865. Madison, WI: Federal Publishing Company, 1908.

Walker, Margaret. *Jubilee.* New York: Mariner Books, 1999.

The War of the Rebellion: A Compilation of the Official Records of the Union and Confederate Armies, Series I, Vol. XXXIV, Part I. Washington, D.C.: Government Printing Office, 1891.

Wascom, Kent. *The Blood of Heaven: A Novel*. New York: Grove Press, 2013.

Wright, J. Leitch Jr. *Florida in the American Revolution*. Gainesville: University Presses of Florida, 1975.

Internet

American Loyalist Claims, 1776–1835. AO 12–13. The National Archives of the United Kingdom, Kew, Surrey, England. Digitized by ancestry.com.

"Bernard G. Farrar, Jr. Collection." University of Missouri Kansas City. https://library.umkc.edu/archival-collections/farrar#.

"Deadliest Public Assembly and Nightclub Fires." National Fire Protection Association. https://www.nfpa.org/Public-Education/Staying-safe/Safety-in-living-and-entertainment-spaces/Nightclubs-assembly-occupancies/Deadliest-public-assembly-and-nightclub-fires.

Ferranti, Seth. "These White People Profited off Their Neighbor's Murder." *Vice*. October 2, 2017. Accessed June 9, 2020. https://www.vice.com/en_us/article/yw3ezv/these-white-people-profited-off-their-neighbors-murder.

Jackson, Jack. "Nolan Expeditions [1791–1801]. Texas State Historical Association: Handbook of Texas. https://www.tshaonline.org/handbook/entries/nolan-expeditions-1791-1801.

Mississippi Project: Yellow Fever Epidemic. Accessed December 16, 2020. http://sites.rootsweb.com/~msalhn/yellowfever.html.

Sabo III, George. "The Natchez Indians." Accessed March 27, 2020. http://archeology.uark.edu/indiansofarkansas/printerfriendly.html?pageName=The%20Natchez%20Indians.

Slave Voyages. Accessed December 20, 2018. http://www.slavevoyages.org/assessment/essays.

"Suicide of Col. McCaleb." *Henry Republic*, April 11, 1878. Accessed through manhattanfirearms.com. http://www.manhattanfirearms.com/McCalebsNavy.html.

Walter Barnes and His Royal Creolians, "Buffalo Rhythm," 1929. Internet Archive. https://archive.org/details/1929-USA-Archives-1929-02-27-Walter-Barnes-And-His-Royal-Creolians-Buffalo-Rhythm.

Newspapers

Brooklyn Times Union
Clarion-Ledger (Jackson, Mississippi)

Courier News (Blytheville, Arkansas)
Delta Democrat-Times
Greenwood Commonwealth (Greenwood, Mississippi)
Long Island Star (New York)
Memphis Daily Appeal
Memphis Public Ledger
Mississippi Free Trader (Natchez)
Natchez Daily Courier
Natchez Democrat
National Gazette
Negro Star
New York Times
Pittsburgh Courier
Shreveport Journal
Simpson County News
St. Louis Globe Democrat
Times-Picayune (New Orleans, Louisiana)
Town Talk (Alexandria, Virginia)
Washington Post
Washington Republican and Natchez Intelligencer (Natchez)
Weekly Mississippian (Jackson, Mississippi)
Winona Times

Other Sources

Bradley, Abraham, William Harrison, and W Barker. Map of the United States, exhibiting the post-roads, the situations, connections & distances of the post-offices, stage roads, counties & principal rivers. Philadelphia: Abraham Bradley, 1804.

Burch, Bryan. *The Rhythm Club Fire* (documentary film). Digital Design House, 2010.

"Inventory of the Estate of John Blommart." American Loyalist Claims, 1776–1835. AO 13. Piece 002. The National Archives of the United Kingdom, Kew, Surrey, England.

"Letter from Col. John Stuart to Henry Stuart." September 5, 1777. American Loyalist Claims, 1776–1835. AO 12–13. The National Archives of the United Kingdom, Kew, Surrey, England.

"The Memorial of John Blommart, Esq." June 24, 1779. American Loyalist Claims, 1776–1835. AO 13. Piece 002. The National Archives of the United Kingdom, Kew, Surrey, England.

About the Authors

Ryan Starrett was birthed and reared in Jackson, Mississippi. After receiving degrees from the University of Dallas, Adams State University and Spring Hill College, as well as spending a ten-year hiatus in Texas, he has returned home to continue his teaching career. He lives in Madison, Mississippi, with his wife, Jackie, and two children, Joseph Padraic and Penelope Rose.

Josh Foreman is from Jackson, Mississippi. His second home is Seoul, South Korea, where he lived, taught, and traveled from 2005 to 2014. He holds degrees from Mississippi State University and the University of New Hampshire. He lives in Starkville, Mississippi, with his wife, Melissa, and his two children, Keeland and Genevieve. He teaches journalism at Mississippi State University.

Visit us at
www.historypress.com